Ethics for a Digital Era

Blackwell Public Philosophy
Edited by Michael Boylan, Marymount University

In a world of 24-hour news cycles and increasingly specialized knowledge, the Blackwell Public Philosophy series takes seriously the idea that there is a need and demand for engaging and thoughtful discussion of topics of broad public importance. Philosophy itself is historically grounded in the public square, bringing people together to try to understand the various issues that shape their lives and give them meaning. This "love of wisdom" – the essence of philosophy – lies at the heart of the series. Written in an accessible, jargon-free manner by internationally renowned authors, each book is an invitation to the world beyond newsflashes and soundbites and into public wisdom.

Ethics for a Digital Era

Deni Elliott

Edward H. Spence

WILEY Blackwell

This edition first published 2018
© 2018 John Wiley & Sons Ltd

The right of Deni Elliott and Edward H. Spence to be identified as the authors of this work has been asserted in accordance with law.

Registered Offices
John Wiley & Sons, Inc., 111 River Street, Hoboken, NJ 07030, USA
John Wiley & Sons Ltd, The Atrium, Southern Gate, Chichester, West Sussex, PO19 8SQ, UK

Editorial Office
9600 Garsington Road, Oxford, OX4 2DQ, UK

For details of our global editorial offices, customer services, and more information about Wiley products visit us at www.wiley.com.

Wiley also publishes its books in a variety of electronic formats and by print-on-demand. Some content that appears in standard print versions of this book may not be available in other formats.

Library of Congress Cataloging-in-Publication Data

Names: Elliott, Deni, author. | Spence, Edward, H. 1949– author.
Title: Ethics for a digital era / by Deni Elliott, Poynter Jamison Chair in Media Ethics and Press Policy, University of South Florida St. Petersburg, US [and] Edward Howlett Spence, School of Communication and Creative Industries, Charles Sturt University, University of Sydney, Australia, 4TU Centre of Ethics and Technology, Netherlands.
Description: First Edition. | Hoboken : Wiley, 2017. | Series: Blackwell public philosophy ; 2357 | Includes bibliographical references and index.
Identifiers: LCCN 2017015034 (print) | LCCN 2017028336 (ebook) | ISBN 9781118968895 (pdf) | ISBN 9781118968901 (epub) | ISBN 9781118968918 (cloth) | ISBN 9781118974667 (pbk.)
Subjects: LCSH: Journalistic ethics. | Online journalism.
Classification: LCC PN4756 (ebook) | LCC PN4756 .E57 2017 (print) | DDC 174/.907–dc23
LC record available at https://lccn.loc.gov/2017015034

Cover image: © Mina De La O/Gettyimages
Cover design: Wiley

Set in 11/14pt Minion by SPi Global, Pondicherry, India
Printed and bound in Malaysia by Vivar Printing Sdn Bhd

10 9 8 7 6 5 4 3 2 1

Contents

Acknowledgments

Deni Elliott: This book is finished with deep appreciation for the University of South Florida, St. Petersburg, for a well-timed research leave when I needed to complete the manuscript, with appreciation for the stellar copyediting and proofreading skills of Pam Hogle, who helped make a book written by two philosophers accessible to students more used to reading tweets, and with thanks for those who gave me physical and mental space to write while I was incidentally homeless during my leave. Thanks also to Amy Landsverk for keeping my Florida home and life in such good shape in my absence. Thanks to Edward Spence for extreme patience as we worked through these concepts and edits.

Edward H. Spence: I would like to acknowledge the following people all of whom to a greater or smaller degree influenced all my work including the current book: to Plato for his constant inspiration who taught me that ideas are everything; my parents, Tom and Dawn Spence, for the freedom they gave me to explore my own ideas and my uncle Edward Howlett Spence, who taught me the value of loyalty and dedication to a worthwhile cause. Though departed, they are never far; to my dear brother Richard Spence who taught me the singular values of courage, humility and integrity, and to my lifelong companion, Kathryn Spence, for her inspiration, insight and patience; my thanks also to the Arts Faculty at Charles Sturt University for a generous Compact grant that allowed me the time to work on this book; and last but not least, my heartfelt thanks to my gracious friend and colleague, Deni Elliott, for being an inspirational co-author of this book. Thank you all. !

Introduction

Writing a book on digital journalism ethics that serves the needs of a twenty-first-century audience and addresses information communication technologies (ICTs) is as complicated as the topic itself. We know that technology will leap forward between the time this book goes to the publisher and when it becomes available to audience members. Even with annual electronic updates, this book will always be at least one step behind the newest device, app, or trending social media site. However, we also know that the fundamental ethical issues that concern journalists and citizens today, such as practices that impact on the truth, reliability, and trustworthiness of communicating information, will apply regardless of technological change. Citizens' need for accuracy will remain as important as it is at present.

Audience members, particularly those born after 1980, are used to embracing the newest communication device, technique, trending site, or story and then moving on when better technology comes along. How we communicate now can change as quickly as the content that we communicate. Today's young adults, who were exposed to communication technologies from the beginning, learned from their early days how to adapt to new devices with new ways to navigate. The logic of software architecture was learned by these users as intuitively as how to crawl and

Ethics for a Digital Era, First Edition. Deni Elliott and Edward H. Spence.
© 2018 John Wiley & Sons Ltd. Published 2018 by John Wiley & Sons Ltd.

take first steps. As we have written an electronic book discussing electronic matters, we generally refer to those reading this book as *users*.

The good news about the study of ethics is that thinking about how people should act in regard to each other and how they should use power in a judicious way predates any technology. Most of the important concepts, issues, and processes for analysis have been part of human practice since our ancestors began living in communal groups. The basic formula for reasoning through ethical issues has been part of Western culture for more than 2,000 years. The ancient Greek philosophers, such as Plato and Aristotle, articulated some basic principles for ethics in private, public, and professional life that have been reinterpreted over the years but that form the basic concepts and principles for the analysis that we use through this day. Today, we call the field of study of how ordinary people should make choices about how to act in the world **practical ethics**. Those basic concepts include the following:

1. Everyone wishes to avoid basic harms like pain, death, and disability for themselves and for those whom they care about;
2. If it is irrational to want to be caused a certain harm in a certain circumstance—that is, there is no good reason for someone wanting to be caused that harm—it is unethical to cause that harm to any other human being;
3. Everyone should be treated justly—they should get what they have a legal right to, what they have an ethical right to, what they deserve, and what they have been promised, and they should not be deprived of what others can get unless there is an ethically relevant justification;
4. People are ethically required to fulfill their role-related responsibilities and to do that without causing unjustified harm to anyone;
5. While people should strive to act in ethically ideal ways by promoting the good and giving extra consideration and care for the most vulnerable, it is ethically required that they do their jobs and do not cause unjustified harm. It is praiseworthy if they act in ethically ideal ways. They are blameworthy if they have failed to meet ethical requirements.

Mass communication ethics, of which digital journalism ethics is a part, has been considered at least since the Greek philosopher Plato wrote the dialogue Gorgias (http://classics.mit.edu/Plato/gorgias.html) in 400 BCE. Plato noticed that some people have the ability to communicate ideas to others and persuade others to hold particular beliefs. He argued that people with the power to communicate and persuade have the ethical requirement to use that power in a way that promotes the public good and that helps make individuals better people.

In the digital era, we can interpret this ancient directive to mean that those who have the power to communicate with mass audiences—that would be anyone with an Internet connection—should use that power to promote good in individuals and community. As we will explore in this book, open and broad communication of ideas generally promotes the good, as compared with the opposite choice of restricting communication. We discuss in this book what it means to communicate in an ethical and responsible manner.

Journalism, at its essence, is the distribution of information so that citizens can make informed and educated decisions for self-governance. Journalism tells users what they need to know and think about if they are going to participate in creating a good community or even simply in living their own lives effectively. Acting corruptly may be effective for certain individuals, and engaging in corruption might advance their financial interests, but it does not benefit society on the whole. That is why corruption is both illegal and unethical. Open communication that leads to transparency and accountability allows for corruption to be detected and disclosed.

The ethics of journalism and the ethics of digital communication more generally, both in the creation and consumption of journalism, serve as the core of *Ethics for a Digital Era*. It is an exciting time to think about journalism ethics and the ethics of digital communication more broadly. The Internet has opened the practice of journalism to everyone with access. There is no topic or opinion or discussion unreachable for the curious user. Every person reading this material electronically literally has the power to change the world. This has resulted in a *convergence* between journalism ethics and communication ethics more broadly, which extends well beyond the traditional boundaries of journalism as previously conceived and practiced. Users of information can also now be creators and communicators of information. Within a different use of the concept of "convergence," Wikileaks (https://wikileaks.org/) is a prime example of such a convergence of digital information, a convergence to which we refer in this book, as a convergence of the communication of information between the 4th Estates (https://en.wikipedia.org/wiki/Fourth_Estate) and 5th Estates (https://en.wikipedia.org/wiki/Fifth_Estate).

Writing about ethics is always an exercise of putting old wine in new bottles. The dilemmas that signal the need to think through ethical questions may change as new technological devices are introduced, but the process of human reasoning and the basic ethical responsibilities of competent, rational adults, whom we will refer to as *moral agents*, remains constant.

Ethics for a Digital Era: Responsible Journalism for Producers and Users must straddle the physical world and the virtual world so that it is useful across platforms. The book contains "old style" in-text citations and a reference list at the end of each chapter for readers who would like to follow up using that method. It also has live hyperlinks for users who are renting or buying this as an e-book and who wish to click back to source additional online material. *Ethics for a Digital Era*, like most contemporary mass communication, must work as a static product but must also be easy to update electronically as new cases, technology, and ideas become available.

We assume that many of this book's users are *digital natives*, people who have grown up comfortably living with one foot in the physical world and the other in the virtual world. Google is older than those who were first-time-in-college at the time of this book's publication. These students have always known a wireless world. Our goal is not to answer all of the ethical questions for journalism in a digital era. Rather, we hope to help users understand ethically relevant aspects of how the practice and products of journalism and the convergent digital media more broadly have changed in the move to the digital era. We provide a method for analyzing issues and demonstrate its use. The questions for reflection at the end of each chapter help users think how they might further apply the topics covered in each chapter. We hope to provide the tools to help users analyze ethical issues in digital journalism and the digital convergent media more generally, wherever they emerge, and we hope to motivate users to use their communication skills to create a better world.

Before proceeding to describe and explain the content of this book a note on *methodology*. This book comprises *three* interrelated components: *ethical and epistemic theory; application of the theory* to digital communication *practices*; and illustration of how the theory applies to those practices by reference to *case studies*. The case studies have been chosen *diachronically* (across time) *rather* than *synchronically* (in the present time) on the basis of important *general types* of illustrative cases. This is for two main reasons.

One reason is to avoid the "currency trap": that is, that only what happens in the present time is important or relevant. That of course is plainly false as that would make most of our knowledge such as for example, Einstein's Theory of Relativity, and other great scientific inventions and discoveries, irrelevant. Some of the historical case studies referred to in this book are significant because of their impact in shaping the ethics of journalism and the ethics digital communication more broadly, especially with regard the media convergence that we discuss in Chapter 6 and elsewhere in this book.

The second reason is to provide a *diachronic* spread of case studies that span the development of journalism and digital communication ethics across time, with an emphasis on *types* of significant cases rather than *tokens* or instances of those types of cases. Our primary purpose for this is to show how the theoretical approach developed in this book, the Dual Obligation Information Theory (DOIT) introduced in Chapter 5, can apply generally to all such cases both now and in the future. To use a metaphor, our hope is to teach our readers the method for catching fish themselves rather than providing them with the caught fish. We expect readers to do some work on their own to connect cases with our arguments of theory and practice and to find other cases that exemplify the concepts explored.

This brings us to two further methodological design features of this book. The first has to do with our choice of *Wikipedia* as a primary source for providing links to further information and readings on relevant topics throughout the book; the second methodological feature has to do with the section on *Questions for Reflection* that we have provided at the end of each chapter of this book.

First, the choice of Wikipedia:

Producing an electronic book with live links is a challenge. Blogs disappear. Content is changed without notice. Archives available today are not available tomorrow. Firewalls block users from accessing primary sources that we used in the process of researching this book. Therefore, many of our hyperlinks take readers to Wikipedia entries. We are confident that this site will be always available and always up-to-date. Wikipedia is not the ultimate research tool, but is a good introduction to a topic that always has a list of vetted sources for further exploration.

When Web 2.0 was in its infancy, many scholars did not consider Wikipedia a credible source as they equated Wikipedia with a physical encyclopedia, but one with no expert control. Even the best researched physical encyclopedias were not considered appropriate sources for scholars or for college students to use as authoritative sources, because encyclopedias simply summarized topics rather than providing primary source material. By analogy, Wikipedia was a secondary, rather than a primary, source. Crowdsourcing was considered to be no substitute for "the truth."

In the years since the 2001 creation of Wikipedia (https://en.wikipedia.org/wiki/Wikipedia), scholars and users have come to recognize that this web site is not a bad, virtual world imitation of a physical encyclopedia. In a 2016 interview on the NPR radio program, On Being (http://www.onbeing.org/program/jimmy-wales-the-sum-of-all-human-knowledge/transcript/8924#main_content).), Wikipedia co-founder Jimmy Wales said that, Wikipedia could boast "15 billion page views a month, 7,000 new articles every day, 80,000 unpaid volunteers worldwide."

Rather than providing a poor model of a twentieth-century encyclopedia, Wikipedia entries are fact-based and evidence-backed and directly point the user to primary sources. Wikipedia has emerged as a model for sharing knowledge through Internet-based democratic action. The site is a model for democracy in three ways:

1. Open access. Wikipedia's mission statement is, "Imagine a world in which every single person on the planet is given free access to the sum of all human knowledge." Access to information is as free as access to the air we breathe in the physical world. The goal is to free information from governmental censorship or corporate control.

2. Difficult dialogues. The structural process of Wikipedia reflects the best of democracy without tyranny of the majority. Every user has the power to create and edit entries on the site. Each creation and edit is reviewed by others. Controversy or disagreement about edits results in dialogue with the shared goal of publishing accurate information. Different perspectives on the same topic can comfortably appear together. Elected administrators have the power to lock sites or block particular users, but all administrative actions are public. Arbitration committees provide binding decisions, including blocking people on both sides of a controversy from contributing to a page.

3. Seeking truth. Crowdsourcing is not equivalent to everyone's opinion being equal. Crowdsourcing is way of removing statements of purported fact from the personality of the provider. Others verify the truth of statements or provide evidence to their falsity. The sources upon which statements depend are available at the end of each article.

Second, the choice of Questions for Reflection:

The primary reason for setting questions for reflection is to strongly encourage the readers to reflect for themselves on the relevant ethical and epistemic principles, their application to the relevant issues and practices and the analysis and evaluation of those issues and practices by reference to illustrative case studies that the readers are also invited to search and discover for themselves. As Aristotle, the ancient Greek philosopher would say, ethical learning, in this case, digital ethics as it applies to the media, comes through individual and group *reflective practice* and not just through the reading of articles and books on the topic. This book therefore encourages constructive *self-learning* through *self- reflection* as an effective and efficient way for becoming a reflective media practitioner.

Ethics for a Digital Era is divided into three parts. *Part One: From Analog to Digital News* which presents the changes related to the move from one-way to interactive mass communication in which users can be both producer and consumer of news. Chapter 1 addresses the paradigm shift that occurred through the technologically induced communication revolution of the latter twentieth century. Chapter 2 describes how legacy news media have adapted to producing news from a web-based platform. Chapter 3 discusses how the web-based platform has created new questions for copyright and how news aggregation has changed news organizations' ability to protect their intellectual property. Chapter 4 argues that the new opportunities that citizens have for accessing information implies a new level of responsibility for them to engage in active citizenship.

Part Two: Thinking Through Ethical Issues in Digital Journalism and Digital Communication more broadly applies a process of normative decision-making to some of the most important issues arising in digital communication in its convergent form that now combines traditional modes of media communication, such as journalism, with new forms of communicating information by non-professional communicators, through the use of blogs, tweets, and other non-traditional communication platforms.

Chapter 5 will show that information has a dual normative structure that commits all disseminators of information to both epistemological (those that relate to knowledge) and ethical norms (those that relate to moral behavior) that are in principle universal and thus global in application. Based on this dual normative characterization of information, the chapter will seek to demonstrate that: information and, specifically, digital information on the Internet, as a process and product of communication, has an inherent normative structure that commits its producers, disseminators, communicators, and users, everyone in fact that deals with information, to certain mandatory epistemological and ethical commitments; and the negligent or purposeful abuse of information in violation of these commitments is also a violation of universal rights to freedom and well-being to which all agents are entitled by virtue of being agents (by agent we mean any person engaged in any purposive activity, such as taking a walk, searching the Internet, writing an essay, etc.,). Chapter 6 examines the phenomenon of converging physical-world static news products with the process-oriented production of web-based news, as well as the broader convergence of information between that produced by professional communicators and non-professional communicators of information. These days, digital information can be created, accessed, disseminated, and used by anyone, anytime, anywhere—worldwide. This change challenges the traditional role and legitimacy of legacy news organizations as the primary and authoritative source of news. This is especially so on matters of public interest. The new world of citizen journalists ranges from the Twitterati (http://www.urbandictionary.com/define.php?term=twitterati) to the WikiLeaks (https://wikileaks.org/index.en.html) founder Julian Assange (https://en.wikipedia.org/wiki/julian_assange).

The primary aim of this chapter is to present a conceptual framework that shows how to examine and evaluate the ongoing transformations wrought by the digitalization of journalism and expansion of its communicators. Specifically, we will seek to show how this conceptual framework allows for the examination and evaluation of the ethics of the ongoing convergence of old and new media at the fundamental level of the *ethics of information*. We will show how this model can be operationalized to evaluate the impact of this convergence and its implications for the social well-being (*the good life*) of individuals and society.

Chapter 7 looks at the ethical issues related to individuals' control over access to themselves or their information. Chapter 8 considers the ethics of information-gathering in the digital era along with what information news providers have a responsibility to publish. Sometimes withholding information is deceptive; sometimes it is not. Chapter 9 examines and explores the presence of corruption in the media by reference to Plato's Myth of Gyges (https://en.wikipedia.org/wiki/Ring_of_Gyges), as this has contemporary significance and relevance in explaining corruption in the media. The primary objective of this chapter is to identify and categorize the different types of media corruption, identify the different ways in which these are caused, and describe the contexts in which they manifest in current physical and virtual media environments and practices.

Part Three: Using the Virtual World to Create a Better Physical World encourages users to bridge their own thinking between the virtual and physical worlds of information and its communication. The previous chapters in the two previous sections focused primarily on identifying and analyzing current practices in digital communication and their ethical implications, and how to prevent or at least minimize unethical practices in digital journalism and digital media communication more broadly. By extension, the chapters in this final section, focus on ethical thinking and practices that not merely prevent unethical conduct, but proactively promote ethical thinking and practice that constitutes moreover, wise thinking and practice in digital media communication.

Chapter 10 investigates the differences between information, knowledge, and wisdom, with the aim examining the significance of those concepts and their relevance for digital media communication. The chapter begins with a short *philosophy play* (Spence 2008) that highlights dramatically those differences and their importance for the dissemination of media information that contributes to our well-being, both as individuals and as a society. The chapter examines how the ethical dissemination of information by journalists and other communicators of digital information more generally, requires both knowledge and wisdom in the form of reflection, understanding, and judgment in knowing when and how to apply knowledge for both the professional and public good. Wisdom is essential because it provides practical guidance for how to act for the enhancement of both personal and social well-being.

Chapter 11 shows how the digital world with its exponential increase in transparency and accountability allows for global understanding and justice to a far greater degree than when users were isolated geographically in the physical world.

Part I
From Analog to Digital News

I

A New Paradigm for News

You don't need to understand the meaning of "paradigm shift" to know that that the last half of the twentieth century witnessed a world-wide communication revolution. The change was so profound that it changed what it means for humans to communicate with one another, interpersonally as well as in mass communication.

This chapter describes the *paradigm shift*—the fundamental change in information production, delivery, and consumption—that occurred in the latter half of the twentieth century. This shift has been called the digital communication revolution (http://www.ojcmt.net/articles/23/237.pdf), the third industrial revolution (https://en.wikipedia.org/wiki/Digital_Revolution), the information age (https://en.wikipedia.org/wiki/Information_Age), and, as we will refer to it in this book, the digital era (http://www.igi-global.com/chapter/digital-era/29024).

The focus of this book is how the creation and consumption of news have changed through this paradigm shift. Examining the changes reveals which practices are mere conventions of this moment in the history of news and which reflect essential values that endure through changes in technology and marketing. By the end of this chapter, users should be able to explain the major ways that the paradigm shift has affected contemporary digital journalism and be able to describe the journalistic values that have transcended paradigm shifts. Users should

Ethics for a Digital Era, First Edition. Deni Elliott and Edward H. Spence.
© 2018 John Wiley & Sons Ltd. Published 2018 by John Wiley & Sons Ltd.

also understand that, throughout history, mass communication in general, and journalism in particular, has experienced a series of paradigm shifts as technology has created new platforms.

A paradigm shift (https://en.wikipedia.org/wiki/Paradigm_shift), according to the scientist who coined that term, Thomas Kuhn (https://en.wikipedia.org/wiki/Thomas_Kuhn), is "a change from one way of thinking to another. It's a revolution, a transformation, a sort of metamorphosis. It does not just happen; rather it is driven by agents of change." Kuhn argues that scientific advancement is not a slow, orderly evolution, but rather is a "series of peaceful interludes punctuated by intellectually violent revolutions," and in those revolutions "one conceptual world view is replaced by another" (Thomas Kuhn, quoted in Take the Leap).

The communication paradigm shift at the end of the twentieth century was as challenging to the status quo as the transportation revolution that changed the world in the first half of that century. In industrialized nations, the first half of the twentieth century saw transition from the horse-and-buggy to trains to planes to at least one automobile in most households. Transportation technologies created a paradigm shift, a change so dramatic that how people behaved in all areas of their lives changed. A 500-mile trip was no longer measured in weeks but in hours. A trip across an ocean could happen in less than a day rather than taking weeks. The new rapid ability to move people and goods expanded commerce, but with the creation of new opportunities, came new problems. For example, people could get fresh foods grown anywhere, rather than consume only those that could be grown seasonally and locally. This resulted in a wider variety of foods available but also created the need to sacrifice taste and ripeness of many fruits and vegetables in favor of their transportability and created a greater carbon footprint per food item. Friends and family no longer needed to live in the same small town to see one another on a regular basis. That expanded career opportunities but separated generations and grown siblings. That limited family members' abilities to babysit children or care for elders.

Limited-access roads, highways, and turnpikes, designed to get people from one point to another as efficiently as possible, were constructed, changing the experience of long-distance ground travel. No longer did drivers need to think about camping on the side of the road or where to find the infrequent roadhouses along the route of travel. Now travelers could select from a multitude of fast foods and easy-access exit-located hotels. Isolated, efficient travel experience triumphed over that found in roadhouse boarding, with communal dining among strangers. Airline and train routes reinforced population and commercial centers, attracting more people and manufacturing by their presence, thus stimulating greater population migration and density. The transportation revolution built upon industry and reinforced the industry-induced change from agrarian to urban lifestyles.

In the last half of the twentieth century, computer and satellite technology created a paradigm shift in communication equal in size and significance to that created by transportation technology. Interpersonal communication that was dependent on physically mailed letters and phone calls that happened to catch a person "in" were replaced with instant verbal and visual messaging, notifying the recipient immediately on a handheld or wearable two-way communication device. News that had been delivered to mass audiences in episodic doses at prescribed times of day changed to immediate, user-initiated access to real-time targeted information. Delivery by a few corporate-owned or government-controlled news organizations that operated within geographical borders gave way to a global flood of information providers and direct interaction between news producers and consumers and a blending of those roles, with no gatekeeping required.

In the twentieth century, those who delivered messages via mass communication were generally professionals. The core group of those who laid claim to the label "journalist" were reporters and editors who worked in print media newsrooms.

Some who worked in the production of radio or television news, including some anchors who delivered the news on camera, field reporters, and producers, considered themselves journalists and worked to uphold professional values. Others who did the same tasks weren't so sure that they were "real" journalists and didn't think that the professionalism expectations of print journalists applied to them. Newspaper photographers and broadcast video and audio recorders were often considered tangential to news reports and were sometimes called "reporters with their brains knocked out" by text-superior colleagues.

Running a machine that captured images or sound was considered inferior to collecting and crafting words into news packages.

Radio shows were hosted by disc jockeys who played phonograph records and read advertising messages and "rip and read (http://www.newscript.com/rip.html)" news bulletins provided by wire services (https://en.wikipedia.org/wiki/List_of_wire_services), with no thought of accountability for the truth or accuracy of the messages that they read.

The notion that stories were best told through a marriage of visuals, text, and sound was still in its infancy.

From the vantage point of today's digital era, it is hard to believe that citizens or leaders in commerce, industry, or government could function without personal computers in hand to provide immediate access to others along with real-time notification of time, weather, and news. In the twentieth century, everyone had a favorite news source. Whether it was the *New York Times, La Monde,* the BBC, or the Australian Broadcasting Corporation depended on location, as each source had limited geographic distribution.

Today, the question, "How do you get your news?" or "How do you know what is going on in the world?" is more likely to elicit the name of a social media app or a dismissive shrug than the name of a legacy news organization. It is disconcerting to anyone with Internet access to consider *not* being able to instantly know what is going on in the world through an infinite variety of sources.

Just as transportation fulfills the goal of physically moving people from one point to another, news production fulfills the goal of giving people information that they need so that they can make educated choices about what they believe, how they can govern themselves, and their role in creating a community that meets their needs and interests. For these goals to be met, essential journalistic values of balance, accuracy, relevance, and completeness must endure.

People seek news for many reasons, including entertainment and interpersonal connection in addition to learning about the world around them. Citizens need to be informed and educated about contemporary events to help them knowledgably participate in self-governance. But no one wants to study the news all of the time. It is logical and ethically acceptable for individuals to sometimes choose not to be informed, just as it is just fine for individuals to sometimes wander through a park with no particular goal of getting from one point to another. But it is impossible to engage in civic life without sometimes seeking news and opinion with the goal of being informed and educated on contemporary issues of the day.

First, Some Definitions

Mass Communication: online *mass communication* is differentiated from interpersonal communication by publisher intent or audience access. If the publisher's intent is to communicate to an unrestricted or unknown audience, or if the site is accessible by an unrestricted or an unknown audience regardless of publisher intent, the message, production, and consumption fall within the realm of mass communication. The creation and consumption of news is one type of mass communication. One may communicate with many different intentions, such as persuasion, sales, or simple expression of opinion. *Ethics for a Digital Era* focuses on the core informational intent and function of journalism: providing and consuming the news.

News: Information counts as news because of a combination of three factors. *News* is a cluster concept (http://itisonlyatheory.blogspot.com/2010/01/cluster-concepts.html). The more elements from each factor a particular piece includes, the more that the particular piece of information counts as *news*. While some pieces are clearly "hard" news and some are clearly pure entertainment or advocacy communication, many examples fall somewhere on the continuum of "more news" to "less news." Opinion pieces, for example, will often contain a few elements from one or more of the three factors of news but will mostly be an argument designed to lead users to share the opinion of the producer. News, on the other hand, tells people what to think *about*, rather telling them what they should conclude. The three factors of news in the digital era are: *(1) publication intent, (2) properties of the product, and (3) user perception.*

(1) Publication intent: the producer of news seeks, synthesizes, and publishes information with the intent of creating an informed and politically literate populace—people who can use the information to make

better-informed choices. Journalistic intent does not imply that all producers of news are objective or have no opinion on the matters that they present. Rather, mass communicators with journalistic intent always have reasons for why they share what they consider to be news. The primary communicative intent, or agenda, for news producers is the belief that "the people" need to know what the producer is about to share. According to media scholars Bill Kovach and Tom Rosenstiel, "For all that the face of journalism has changed, indeed, its purpose has remained remarkably constant, if not always well-served, since the notion of 'a press' first evolved more than three hundred years ago....The primary purpose of journalism is to provide citizens with the information they need to be free and self-governing" (Kovach and Rosenstiel 2011, 12). The principles that separate those who have journalistic intent from those who don't are the values of verification, independence, and accountability.

(2) Properties of the product: News is information that can be used for self-governance. Information that can be used for self-governance can be as pragmatic as being told that a bridge over which one drives home is closed for repair. It can be as complicated and multidimensional as various views from policy makers and topic experts on health-care or defense strategy or immigration policies. It is as relevant, or irrelevant, to the individual voter as the religion or sexual orientation of a candidate for public office. These properties are commonly considered to differentiate news stories from other types of informative nonfiction writing:

a. Significant impact on the user;
b. Alerts users to events or issues that have significant impact on other people;
c. Geographical closeness to the user;
d. Timeliness, in that recent events are more newsworthy than less-recent events;
e. Conflict that is person-to-person or person to nature, government, or organization;
f. Peculiarity or unusualness;
g. Prominence, in that better-known people are more likely to be newsworthy.

Every production that is intended to be an example of news will include one or more of these properties.

(3) User perception: In the twenty-first century, the user's perception matters in a whole new way in determining what counts as news. In the pre-digital past, news was dispersed to the broadest possible audience. As different audience members started out with more knowledge of a subject than other audience members, some people got far more detail than they needed and some got far less than they needed. Now, individuals can easily seek information from a variety of sources, so news producers can target a more defined audience and repackage news to meet the needs of different users. No one can know everything, but adults living in community have both the need and the responsibility to seek out information that allows them to engage in civic life. The expression, "That's news to me!" has taken on a more literal meaning than ever before. Self-governing citizens need to be on the lookout for bits of information that may be insignificant to some people, but that, nevertheless, can change that individual's overall world-view and ways of functioning. Citizens now have the ability to easily access what they need to know to engage with others in their communities.

Legacy news organizations: institutions that published news through print, radio, or television prior to the digital age are called legacy news organizations. Major legacy news organizations survived the transition from the "news cycle" to digital publication. The pre-digital age required specific deadlines by which information needed to be collected so that it could be processed and delivered at particular broadcast news program times or in newspapers delivered each morning or evening to audience members at their homes or to stores for single-issue sales. Surviving legacy news organizations have joined the legions of web-based information providers in thinking first of dispersing information as close to real time as possible through their web sites. Some legacy news organizations have retained accompanying print or broadcast editions; others have not. For this book's purposes, web-based communication is assumed to be the sustaining model for twenty-first-century news production, delivery, and consumption.

Ethics: the study of how moral agents do, and how they should, act in regards to other people, non-human subjects of moral worth, and natural systems is called ethics. *Moral agents* are competent, rational adults who can be held accountable for their voluntary actions. The minimal ethical requirement is for moral agents to meet their role-related responsibilities and do so without causing unjustified harm to other people, animals, or natural systems. Ethical imperatives of mass communication in the pre-digital, twentieth-century model were based on a shared acceptance of professional values among those who produced the news. The ethical imperatives of twenty-first-century mass communication must be based instead on how people should act in regard toward one another, regardless of what professional title the producer or sharer of information may choose to use. There is no practical restriction in the digital era between who can provide information with journalistic intent and who cannot.

The New World of News Production and Consumption

The chart that follows illustrates three major differences in news under the old paradigm as compared with the new paradigm. A description of each change follows the table, along with ethical implications of those changes. The paradigm shift from professionally mediated, one-way news to user-chosen, interactive news has necessitated a change in how consumers, practitioners, and scholars think about ethical guidelines for mass communication.

Old paradigm	New paradigm
Physical news products	Virtual, dynamic news production
Practitioner control	User control
Accidental information acquisition by exposure to a collection of unrelated stories	Additional information acquisition through hyperlinks in a particular story

Physical news products to virtual dynamic news production: in the twentieth-century model, news pieces were produced and then held in their print or broadcast form. In the twenty-first century, news pieces are published on the web as soon as they are deemed "ready" by the news producer; they may continue to evolve as new facts become known and inaccuracies are discovered.

Journalistic truth is different from scientific truth in that scientific truths are generalizable and static. The rules of nature are consistent. They apply the same, wherever on earth one happens to be. Gravity works the same now as it did 20, 200, and 2,000 years ago. Gravity is a truth that will not change.

Journalistic truths evolve. News is the sharing of episodic stories. News presents snapshots of events and issues and people. As with snapshots taken over time, the events, issues, and people that populate a news piece may look different in each new presentation. But, once news was delivered in the pre-digital era in archival form, such as a television broadcast or a daily newspaper, the story could be saved in the format published and then found, reviewed, and compared to later editions.

Under the new paradigm, as web-based postings can be easily changed by their publishers, more unverified claims are published, and comparisons with earlier editions are more difficult. The hours between gathering facts and publishing in the pre-digital era provided time for reporting and fact-checking. In the digital era, users are looking for real-time publication, and publishers feel pressure to get out information *now*.

Information may be distributed without fact-checking.

When previous digital versions of a news story are simply overwritten to present the most current, accurate account with no indication of change, two ethical problems arise. First, there may be historical significance in how a situation was first understood that will be lost if previous versions are not preserved and easy to find. Next, even though a story's publisher can easily extract elements or add new copy to a story without readers knowing of the change, the initial publications will certainly be cached in some recipients' devices. It may not be evident, when readers access evolving versions of a story, how small facts in the story have changed. Audience members may think that they are looking at the same story that they initially saw, as it has the same headline and same picture, but there may be significant differences in the textual content. Making significant changes in a story without notice to readers is an ethical issue because readers may believe an earlier version of a story and use it as a basis for action. Acting on false beliefs can cause direct or indirect harms to the user of information.

Practitioner control to user control: Under the old paradigm, gatekeeping was a primary and important function of news production. News producers decided which of the myriad events and issues were most "newsworthy" and how those newsworthy events should be framed. The way that events were prioritized in the publication helped audience members understand how and why the event or issue was important.

Audience members—the users of mass communication—are now their own gatekeepers. Search engines allow users to find information with the entry of a keyword. Users can create their own news packages by picking individual stories from among an array of online offerings, including social networking, reviews, and affinity-focused topic sites, along with sites that deliver more traditional-looking journalistic accounts of events. Users let aggregators and news sites know, through their choices, which topics are of most interest to them. Now, news providers can know, in real time, which stories are having impact and how much impact they are having as their web sites count visitors and measure the amount of time that visitors spend on pages within their sites. News providers use this feedback to determine which stories users think are important, and they may choose to expend additional reporting resources on those topics that matter most to users. Users also have the opportunity to provide content-rich feedback by offering reader comments to the news producer. They can participate in discussions with other readers on news or social media sites and offer their own perception to the stories of the day. The rich variety of news sources creates an ethical issue because users have a new level of responsibility to seek out important, accurate information. Just as food diets need to include appropriate nutrition, information diets need to include exposure to fact and a diversity of opinion so that citizens can understand what is really going on in their communities and the world. Otherwise, they are likely to act on false beliefs.

Change in accidental information: under the old paradigm, professional journalists laid out a newspaper in different sections, with stories prioritized by location and length. On the front page, readers could expect to find what the gatekeepers determined to be the most important stories of the day. On the inside, they found interesting, but less urgent, stories. Readers were exposed to information that they would not have known or cared about simply because it was there. In looking for stories that matched their interest, they would see headlines about matters that they might not have known to look for. Television and radio broadcasts followed a similar format, with the most important stories being the longest and nearest to the start of the program. Viewers and listeners knew when to expect the broadcast of what journalists believed to be the most important stories. People "accidentally" acquired information because it was published near something in which they already had interest.

In the new paradigm, users may customize their news feeds so that they get no international news or no news about politics. On the other hand, they may easily dig deep into context and research beneath the reporting of surface facts. This is an ethical issue because of the role-related responsibility of citizens to engage with the community in which they live. Digging deeper into a subject of interest may make an individual knowledgeable but not broadly informed. Making good decisions for self-governance depends on citizens being informed about the contemporary events and situations likely to affect them. That means that individuals must look beyond their initial interests and work intentionally to learn the important news of the day.

Under the old paradigm, users were exposed to stories that they didn't expect. The front page of a broadsheet newspaper had headlines and at least a few hundred words that introduced between four and eight stories; the stories were then "jumped" to an inside page.

Now, users may be delivered stories in the categories of their interest. They may not be exposed to stories outside of their interest. However, through hyperlinks or keyword searches, they can easily explore available background and context.

Under the old paradigm, exposure was broad but shallow. Audience members had only the information that was offered by the news provider. Under the new paradigm, exposure is narrow but deep. News seekers are less likely to be exposed to a rich variety of topics or a variety of opinion unless they purposefully seek these out. While news seekers under the old paradigm could depend on a news organization to provide exposure to important contemporary issues, now they have to responsibility to seek those out. Citizens have both the opportunity and the responsibility to be more active in seeking out information that educates them for self-governance.

A Brief History of Journalism Ethics and Paradigm Shifts

Discussions of responsible mass communication have gone on for as long as people have relayed messages to groups. From early cave and cliff carvings and paintings, it is safe to say that humans from a very early time had an innate need tell their stories in a way that could be shared broadly and preserved. But for thousands of years, human growth and development took place without widely shared, mediated knowledge. Mass publication was limited by the hand or block lettering or pictorials required to produce it and by illiteracy of the general populace.

In an early treatise on the topic, Gorgias (http://classics.mit.edu/Plato/gorgias.html), a dialogue written by the Greek philosopher Plato, we find the philosopher Socrates in roughly 400 BCE stating that those who have the power to persuade others must do so with intent of leading those listening to truth and goodness. Socrates says, "So this is what that skilled and good orator will look to when he applies to people's souls whatever speeches he makes....He will always give his attention to how justice may come to exist in the souls of his fellow citizens and injustice be gotten rid of, how self-control may come to exist there and lack of discipline be gotten rid of, and how the rest of excellence may come into being there and evil may depart" (Plato). Socrates points out that the character of the speaker matters as well as the message. He asks rhetorically, "Shouldn't we then attempt to care for the city and its citizens with the aim of making the citizens themselves as good as possible? For without this…it does no good to provide any other service if the intentions of those who are likely to make a great deal of money or take a position of rule over people or some other position of power aren't admirable and good" (Plato). Some might argue that informing the public is different from the notion of people of good character providing messages that are intended to create "the good" in others. We return to the notion of ethically ideal journalism later in this book.

Acta diurna, translated from Latin as "Daily Proceedings," was a hand-lettered public notice tacked up in locations within the Roman Empire beginning as early as 60 BCE. *Tching-pao*, Palace News, a woodblock printed official publication of the Chinese T'ang dynasty appeared in public locations before 1000 CE. These are examples of early printed versions of mass communication. While expensive and slow to create, printed news had a permanence that made it superior to the oral tradition that had previously sustained mass communication.

A paradigm shift in mass communication occurred in Germany in the mid-1450s, when Johannes Gutenberg invented the printing press. News delivery became entwined with technology and marketing forevermore. While the printing and mass distribution of newssheets transferred power from government officials to citizen publishers, the first evident transfer of power through communication technology was in the tightly controlled religious structure of the time in Europe.

Before the invention of the printing press, important religious books, such as hand-lettered Bible, Torah, and Koran, available only to the wealthy and religiously approved few, were read to the faithful and interpreted by religious leaders. With the invention of the printing press, cheaper, printed copies of these important books became available for direct reading and interpretation by individuals. Print communication's new reach challenged the systems of economic and ecclesiastic control held by religious organizations. For example, the Gutenberg press destroyed the system of paid "indulgences" that brought significant income to the church. Indulgences, which required days of careful hand-lettering by monks, were bought by Christians to secure the passage of recently dead relatives from purgatory to heaven. Suddenly, with the new technology, printing presses could create, within hours, hundreds of indulgences.

Once indulgences were produced mechanically and quickly, the church lost money. Hand-lettered missives were no longer required. Printers made money. The cheaper indulgences were handed over to the church to save souls, at a financial savings to the penitents. It is not a coincidence that religious leaders stopped selling such passages from purgatory to heaven when such sales no longer resulted in financial gain for the church (Eisenstein 1979).

The first newspaper produced independently of government or religion was probably the *Gazette de France,* published in Paris in 1631. In both Germany and France, as reporting was produced by entrepreneurial press owners, the fourth estate was born. When London's *Daily Universal Register* published dispatches from reporters at the site of conflict during the Napoleonic Wars at the turn of the nineteenth century, citizens were able to read, for the first time, news about military battles that did not come from governmental sources. A similar tradition simultaneously developed in the North American Colonies in the late 1700s, as James Franklin and his brother, Benjamin, published the *New England Courant* and *Pennsylvania Gazette,* respectively, telling stories from the Colonists' point of view, rather than from that of the King of England. The importance that such newspapers played in successful revolutionary rhetoric led the founders of the newly formed United States to guarantee press freedom as part of the First Amendment to the US Constitution.

Print journalism enjoyed 200 years as an activist, revolutionary pursuit in Australia, England, Europe, and the United States. The oral tradition of credible or eloquent leaders telling the stories of important events and issues to mass audiences gave way to the superiority and consistency of stories created by reporters who observed the relevant action and told stories without the garnish of governmental spin. Printed news showed its ability to stimulate public action and response. The role-related responsibility of news organizations was born: the special job of journalism is to ignore the pressure of special interests, including government or even the journalists' own biases, in order to provide citizens with accurate, verifiable, and independently produced information that they need for self-governance.

Throughout the 1800s, the proliferation of printing press owners provided vehicles for advertising by local businesses. Advertising set off the costs of production, which allowed publishers to lower their prices to reach a mass rather than elite audience. The penny press (https://en.wikipedia.org/wiki/Penny_press) was descriptive in that news was now available to everyone at the cost of a mere penny. News providers worked to appeal to larger, less-elite audiences, with greater circulation used to increase their charges to advertisers. The accessibility of these newspapers increased literacy and provided a shared, mediated knowledge of important events in the community, nation, and world.

However, a symbiotic relationship between publishers and advertisers quickly formed, creating an early conflict of interests as publishers struggled to meet the needs of audience members and fulfill the demands of advertisers. Publishers wanted to separate editorial content from advertising, but advertising got the bigger and better display. Advertisers exerted pressure to control editorial content so that it did not threaten sales of their goods or services. Publishers sometimes stood up to these economic pressures—and sometimes adjusted their editorial standards to keep the advertiser money flowing.

The penny press was dismissed as "yellow journalism" by the elite press. These inexpensive newspapers induced the more-elite papers to highlight their higher standards and professionalism.

As the nineteenth century drew to a close, the professionalism of journalism was about to begin. The University of Missouri (https://journalism.missouri.edu/jschool/) boasts the oldest journalism school in the country, dating back to 1908. Joseph Pulitzer, founded the Columbia University Graduate School of Journalism (https://en.wikipedia.org/wiki/Columbia_University_Graduate_School_of_Journalism) in 1912. Journalists from elite newspapers, such as the *New York Times* and *Washington Post*, formed the first professional guild, first called the Sigma Delta Chi fraternity, now called The Society of Professional Journalists (https://www.spj.org/).

The invention of the telegraph at the turn of the nineteenth to the twentieth century provided another convergence of technology, economics, and the ethics of journalism, creating the first major paradigm

shift in mass communication in 500 years. At the time that these technologies were in development, the industrial revolution and unending
series of scientific discoveries gave people a new sense of control over
their environment. Causes and effects and solutions to problems could
all be discovered, if only enough talent and resources were dedicated to
the problem. Truth was believed to be external, certain, and knowable.
These beliefs about the world and human ability to control nature
through knowledge reverberated in the twentieth-century journalistic
paradigm.

The elite news organizations, which had financial and human
resources, were quick to capitalize on the telegraph's ability to transmit
news to multiple destinations across long distances. Individual news
organizations pooled their resources to create co-ops, called wire associations, which sent material to the members first via telegraph, then using
telephone lines, then satellite. The wire associations, which United Press
International (UPI) (http://www.upi.com/) and Associated Press (AP)
(http://www.ap.org/) exemplify, hired journalists to transmit information
(first text, then photographs, then audio and video) from distant scenes
to the multitude of member news organizations. Transmitted product
had to have true mass appeal; the stories could not be targeted toward
audience members with particular political ideologies or regionally
cultural perspectives. But the focus was often to reach the readers to
whom advertisers marketed—those in wealthy dominant society.

As the audience members that advertisers most wished to reach were
members of the wealthy dominant society—Euro-Americans serving as
the prototype—journalists and news organizations produced news to
appeal to these consumers instead of reaching out to diverse citizens.
The blander-the-better, appeal-to-the-wealthy news products made the
best economic sense. Prompted by technology and marketing considerations, not ethical principles, the "objective" news stories nevertheless
became the ethical standard for journalism, standing in comparison to
the sensationalism of the local, popular, tabloid press.

In 1923, the American Society of Newspaper Editors created the
first Code of Ethics for Journalism (http://ethics.iit.edu/ecodes/
node/4457), exemplifying the technical and scientific view of people in

the industrialized nations in the new century. Journalists were expected to have "natural and trained powers of observation and reasoning." The primary role of the journalist was that of "chronicler."

Newspapers' codes of ethics echoed that belief through mid-century, including the *New York Times* in the 1960s, "Although total objectivity may be impossible because every story is written by a human being, the duty of every reporter and editor is to strive for as much objectivity as humanly possible.... presenting both sides of the issue is not hedging but the essence of responsible journalism," and the St. Paul *Pioneer Press* and St. Paul *Dispatch*, at around the same time, said it this way, "One of a newspaper's major functions is to be a mirror of the society in which it exists."

The principle of objective reporting contrasted with biased, sensationalized, and sometimes blatantly false reporting in the penny press of the 1800s, which was carried into the 1900s by the tabloids. The process of objective reporting was found to create a barrier that interfered with journalists' ability to meet their role-related responsibility of telling citizens what was needed for self-governance.

Reporting on World War II and the reporting that followed through the latter half of the twentieth century illustrates this. World War II was not a controversial war, from the point of view of Australia, the British Commonwealth, and the United States. The UK and Australia had been involved in direct combat since the late 1930s. When the United States finally entered the war in response to the Japanese attack on Pearl Harbor, its military base in Hawaii, all but one US representative voted approval. Few citizens questioned the legitimacy of WWII. As there was perceived to be only one "right" perspective on that war, reporting was relatively uncontroversial. The war reporting also allowed for the application of new technologies.

When Pearl Harbor was attacked on December 7, 1941, America's entrance into the war was a radio news exclusive from 2:22 p.m. Eastern Standard Time, when the first wire service report described the destruction of air force carriers, fighter planes, and the military that manned them. This was the first crisis broadcast for the American public in real time. Longer, explanatory newspaper stories were not available until daybreak the following day.

As the war progressed, CBS correspondent Edward R. Murrow gave listeners minute-by-minute descriptions of life in the war zone, mostly reporting from Europe. He experimented with new reporting techniques. Listeners were introduced to what we now call "natural sound"; they could hear the bombs falling for themselves. They heard what was going on at the scene while Murrow described and interpreted it for them.

For the three years and nine months that the US military fought in WWII, hundreds of US reporters on battlefronts around the world created radio, print, photography, and motion-picture reports for an eager American public.

Within a decade of the war's end, however, objectivity and the news came under serious attack. The United States returned to peacetime secure in its military strength but not as sure of the country's ability to withstand the more subtle threat of anti-democratic politics.

Communism was an intellectual curiosity to some and a viable political alternative to others. But the concern that Communists were plotting to overthrow the US government grew, particularly among those in government. The House Un-American Activities Committee and Senator Joseph McCarthy's permanent Senate subcommittee on investigations in the early 1950s drew media attention through the drama of unsubstantiated political claims.

McCarthy exploited the conventions of objective reporting. The news cycles of the time revolved around daily deadlines for newspaper publication. McCarthy's claims of Communists infiltrating the US government, the press, the armed forces, and the entertainment industry gained credibility thanks to the "chronicle" style of journalism that was prized at the time.

Day after day, the senator announced his new set of allegations just before newspapers' deadlines. There was no time for journalists to find an equally credible source who might give an opposing view to McCarthy's claims. The news convention of the day was that journalists reported only what they were told by named, credible sources. The senator provided the illusion of expertise and knowledge. Thus the journalists repeated what the senator said. They could include denials from those he charged in the next day's or in the next week's publications, but those denials did not have the same impact as the publication of the senator's continual, unanswered charges.

Thoughtful journalists were troubled that their conventional style of reporting did not get the truth out to citizens. Journalists knew, but could not find a way to say in the news columns, that Senator McCarthy's allegations of communist ties were often false and his pronouncement of the sweeping Red Tide of Communism was dramatic but not true.

It took the maverick television reporting of Edward R. Murrow to provide context to McCarthy's allegations. The just-born television documentary had not yet developed norms of conduct, as had printed news publications. The television story was different enough from a newspaper story that television journalists didn't think that they had to follow the same rules. Rather than be dependent on what credible sources had to say, as were the newspapers of the time, the content of television news was controlled by the producer. Television documentaries included taped interviews with sources, but the producer who wrote the full script for the story and the reporter/anchor who verbally wove the sources and visuals together did not hesitate to clarify or interpret for the television audience. The *See It Now* piece that demonstrated the falsity of McCarthy's charges aired in early March 1954. In the end, McCarthy fell victim to the reporting process that he had himself exploited. The *See It Now* program provoked public disgust at the senator's misuse of power and of news media. McCarthy's denial and explanation, aired four weeks later, could not rally attention or belief that could stand up to Murrow's exposure of him. It was also clear that Senator McCarthy, as passionate as he was about his crusade to rid the United States of Communists, did not have the charisma or credibility of the well-known, well-loved war hero and broadcast celebrity, Edward R. Murrow. McCarthy was disgraced, and the journalist as credible source was born.

The Civil Rights movement followed in the 1950s and the 1960s. As the events and issues of desegregation erupted on the streets of Birmingham, Alabama, as well as in the halls of the US Supreme Court, journalists realized that they often could not find a matched pair of equally prominent sources who represented opposite points of view.

There was the powerful status quo of some Southern statesmen declaring that "separate but equal" was good enough for African-Americans. And there were the voiceless and relatively powerless African-American citizens, led by an eloquent minister, Dr. Martin Luther King, asking for what the US Constitution seemed to guarantee for all citizens: equal protection under the law. The principles of objective reporting do not play out so easily with this complicated public policy story. Simply presenting external events and what people involved with the events said did not produce adequate reporting. Issues and events needed to be explained. Visuals, like law enforcement officials blasting demonstrators with fire hoses and K9 units allowing their dogs to threaten young children in the street, told a story that could not be "balanced" by presenting a view that such actions were justified. Journalists found that the real story was found in the how they wove together who was saying and doing what.

The war in Vietnam, too, signaled problems for the reporter-as-conduit style of reporting. Reflecting national ambivalence and ultimately amplifying anti-war sentiment, news coverage undoubtedly promoted a lack of public support for US military actions. Television coverage of the battlefields brought the scenes of death and destruction to American households just as citizens prepared their evening meals. Whether intentionally or not, journalism played an important role in the formation of public policy and public action relating to the Vietnam War.

The assumptions that sustained the old paradigm of journalism were crumbling. Among those assumptions was the belief that a balanced story is one that equally represents two opposing points of view. This ultimately reduced the reporter to striving to be nothing more than a clear channel for sources who had polarizing points of view. The framing technique used—an attempt to balance of perspectives—was based on the misperception that every story had two equal sides. News organizations often lost a story's nuance by framing controversial topics as competitions between powerful points of view. Most stories have many sides; some have only one. There are no opposing perspectives when reporting on the devastation caused by a hurricane. When stories are framed to provide polarized opposing points of view, the true story is often lost.

Any hope that journalism might return to some mythical earlier day and settle for unobtrusively relaying easily discoverable news items to readers and viewers disappeared in the two years of reporting on Watergate. This was a story in which reporting intentionally intruded into the story's development and creation. It was one of investigative reporting's finest hours.

The ever-evolving news story that culminated in the resignation of President Richard M. Nixon on August 9, 1974, was rich with political importance and filled with the twists of a good crime novel. The story could not have been told if journalists had stuck to reporting within the old paradigm.

Two novice reporters for the *Washington Post*, Bob Woodward and Carl Bernstein, did not wait for official pronouncements or for on-the-record credible sources to tell the nation what was happening and why. Woodward and Bernstein obtained information however they could, tricking telephone company clerks and pressuring witnesses called before the grand jury into disclosing information to them.

Woodward and Bernstein were not the first reporters to find that they could produce more accurate reporting by stepping outside the lines of conventional professional values and practices, but they were the first to do so in such a sustained, public, and successful way that generations of journalism students wanted to follow in their footsteps, regardless of the lessons they learned in ethics classes.

Rather than searching for, finding, and then reporting some indisputable truth, the Watergate reporting included the creation of a story constructed like a jigsaw puzzle from a confluence of perspectives emerging from White House statements, leaked audio tapes, insiders seeking to expose corruption, those seeking to cover it up, those changing sides, illegally leaked grand jury testimony, testimony before the US House, and files from local law enforcement pieced together with others obtained from the FBI.

Journalistic lore holds that Woodward and Bernstein established and held to a "two source" rule—they would never report anything unless they had that information verified by two independent sources. It is unlikely that they always followed this rule.

If every claim published during the reporting of Watergate had the backing of two independent sources, one would be forced to conclude that, after President Nixon and then-Secretary of State Henry Kissinger knelt together in prayer in the Oval Office in the presence of only one another during the Watergate crisis, either one of them or close confidants of theirs, confirmed this intimate moment for the journalists. It is far easier to believe that Woodward and Bernstein drew conclusions from a conglomerate of sources "close to the matter" and constructed a narrative that best fit the pieces that they were able to collect.

Remnants of the old paradigm could be seen through the end of the twentieth century, despite the undeniable pressure to move to a different kind of journalism. For example, the attempt to establish a national health-care system in the United States in 1994 was reported by mainstream media as a political debate between the administration of President Bill Clinton and the Republican-controlled Congress. The story of the need for uninsured citizens to access needed health care was overpowered by the win-lose style of the policy story's presentation. It took more than another decade before the public issue of developing a new health-care policy could be discussed without the goal of providing health care to uninsured citizens getting lost in media's attempt to frame the story from an either/or perspective.

The pillars of the new paradigm are immediacy and interactivity. The challenge for credible news media is to retain standards of reporting that separate them from self-interested or less-competent information givers and to use new technology to enhance the important journalistic voice.

Owing to the availability of a constant stream of information from many sources, with consumers adding pieces to the information puzzle or providing commentary as the story evolves, a news story can become a never-ending story, with little financial investment by the news organization. Credibility is found in the judgment of the news managers publishing in the virtual and physical world, as they choose among the variety of voices and video and add in their own professional perspective to create a comprehensive, but constantly changing, narrative. Those that consistently tell the accurate story of the moment gain credibility and the trust of their users.

Marketing, as well as technology, helped construct and sustain the ethical principles that supported the old paradigm of journalism; similarly, a new technologically-driven and market-driven set of possibilities and objectives are helping to define the ethical principles that support and sustain journalistic practice within the new paradigm.

The world has changed through the information revolution. Responsibilities for producers and users of news have changed. Journalism ethics can no longer be based solely on ideals of professionalism. As we are all in this together now, journalism ethics that serves current and future audiences is, like that of the distant pre-printing-press past, based on the precepts of common morality. Whatever their title, people who have the power to communicate are ethically required to do so responsibly.

Questions for Reflection

1 *Identify how the digital era has created a paradigm shift for interpersonal communication.*

2 *How have forms of mass communication other than journalism (such as persuasion, advertising, entertainment) been affected by the communication revolution?*

3 *Describe some ways that news providers can be transparent about changes that they make to web-published articles.*

4 *How can citizens encourage one another to become informed about important contemporary issues of the day? Where would you look to get exposed to issues that you might not otherwise know about? What makes that source of news a credible source?*

5 *How is Wikipedia different from the printed encyclopedias of the past? Does edited crowd-sourcing result in more accurate and complete presentation of information as compared with professionally written pieces? Why or why not?*

Works Cited

Kovach, B. and T. Rosenstiel. 2011. *The Elements of Journalism*. New York: Three Rivers Press.

Plato. "Gorgias." The Internet Classics Archive. Accessed November 10, 2015. http://classics.mit.edu/Plato/gorgias.html.

Take the Leap. "What Is a Paradigm Shift?" Accessed February 5, 2015. http://taketheleap.com/define.html.

2

Legacy News Organizations Move from Analog to Digital

"Fall in Love for a Good Cause (http://www.nytimes.com/2007/11/04/fashion/04match.html?_r=0)," published by the *New York Times* November 4, 2007, was one of the many feel-good profiles of philanthropist-matchmaker Pari Livermore that appeared in local and national media around that time. According to the *Times*, Livermore "has facilitated the *affaire de coeur* for a number of high-profile singles: a hedge fund executive, a beauty pageant winner, a neurologist, even a princess… [S]he asks those who seek her assistance to donate money or time to one of a dozen or so charities… she finds about 100 women who, instead of donating large sums, volunteer to be on a committee for Ms. Livermore's Red & White Ball, a singles charity event held every other year in San Francisco that attracts up to 1,000 attendees" (Rosenbloom 2007).

Fast-forward to the summer of 2015 when Nancy Levine, a single executive recruiter looking for love, reached out to Livermore. Levine had found Livermore through a Google search and was impressed by the parade of prestigious publications touting Livermore's unusual approach of demanding philanthropy, rather than a fee, from her successful and wealthy clientele. Levine passed Livermore's initial tests for beauty and success. But when Livermore asked Levine to send a $1,000 donation to her home address for her favorite charity, Spotlight on Heroes, Levine decided to dig deeper.

Ethics for a Digital Era, First Edition. Deni Elliott and Edward H. Spence.
© 2018 John Wiley & Sons Ltd. Published 2018 by John Wiley & Sons Ltd.

Levine discovered that Spotlight on Heroes was not recognized as a charity by federal or state law. Where checks made out to Spotlight ended up was a mystery. Levine contacted the *New York Times*, the most influential of the publications that had touted Livermore's credentials and philanthropy. In her complaint to *NYT* executive editor Dean Baquet, Levine wrote, "It took me 15 minutes to research and find that her charity has never been a charity. I think the *New York Times* may want to consider re-examining its 'glowing profile' of Ms. Livermore in light of the facts" (Levine 2007).

Further investigation by Levine and the online news providers that Levine contacted, *BuzzFeed* and the *Daily Beast*, suggested that Spotlight and The Red & White Ball, which the *New York Times* called a "charity event," had not met legal filing requirements. This fact could have been easily found by the *Times* reporter before that newspaper published the 2007 profile of Livermore.

When *BuzzFeed* reporter Kendall Taggart asked Livermore in 2015 about Spotlight's registrations and tax filings, Livermore pleaded ignorance. "I'm a great fundraiser," she said, "but not a good business-woman." In that interview, Livermore said she raised $50,000 or so dollars for Spotlight on Heroes, but that was only a small percentage of the millions that she claimed that she had gathered for other charities over the past thirty years. When she was asked to show how much money Spotlight on Heroes had distributed and to whom, Livermore declined, citing first a concern for her clients' privacy and then…the health of her husband, whom, she said, "has been extremely ill" (Taggart 2015).

BuzzFeed also checked out a few other purported facts from the published profiles on Livermore. "An article in the *San Francisco Examiner* said that she received an undergraduate degree from New York University and a master's degree in literature from the University of California at Berkeley…But both universities say they have no record of either Pari Livermore or Pari Caldwell, her name at birth" (Taggart 2015).

Of the half-dozen media outlets that had done positive profiles of Livermore in 2007–2008 and that were then provided evidence by Levine years later showing where their previous stories went wrong, only one, the *Marin Independent Journal*, did a follow-up story. And, although the positive years'-old profiles continued to be featured on Livermore's web sites and pop up high in Google searches in the fall of 2015, none of the media had attached corrections to their original online stories.

The *New York Times* public editor, Margaret Sullivan, published an acknowledgement of Levine's concern in her column of November 13, 2015, four months after Levine's initial contact with the *Times*. In it, Sullivan wrote, "When I first heard about the new information about Ms. Livermore, I sent it to a couple of *Times* editors, thinking that there might be a follow-up story here. That didn't happen. While I under-stand the reluctance to go back eight years to amend an article (and the floodgates that might open if every article is treated this way), I do think that it's worth noting this information somewhere. Again, I can't call for a correction since there's no specific factual error to correct. But it's not ideal that the glowing profile stands as the only *Times* reference to Ms. Livermore's record and background, given the developments. Perhaps this post, with its highly searchable headline, will help" (Sullivan 2015).

Three weeks after Sullivan's publication, the public editor's acknowl-edgement surfaced on front Google page in a search for Pari Livermore (https://www.google.com/webhp?sourceid=chrome-instant&ion=1&espv=2&ie=UTF-8#q=%22Pari+Livermore%22).

New Ethical Issues for a Virtual Environment

Because stories now live on eternally on the Internet, news organiza-tions are faced with the problem of whether to make corrections on stories that remain in public view long after the initial reporting was done. In the days of analog publication, newspapers ran corrections as soon as news managers became aware of a substantial problem in a pub-lished story. Television news programs published on-air corrections of substantial errors in their broadcast stories, generally at the end of a show as soon as they learned about the error. Corrections ran as close as possible to the time of the initial publication.

Now, search engines keep stories easy to access years after publication. Skeptical information users like Nancy Levine may do better research than the initial reporters. Others might remain unaware of any information beyond a positive, but false, account. This has created a quandary for news managers who thought that their jobs were done once a story was published and had not immediately generated evidence of error. News managers perceive various obstacles to correcting a published error after the fact: first, the first story may have been accurate at the time, but facts unavailable at the time of initial reporting, may have surfaced. As journalism publishes evolving, rather than static, truth (see, for example, Elliott 1996 (http://digifolio.me/elliott/wp-content/uploads/sites/41/2012/05/Journalistic-Research1.pdf)), it is not reasonable to expect news organizations to update stories that were true at the time after initial publication. Second, errors that seem insignificant, particularly after a long passage of time, may not be worth the cost of staff hours to process an update.

This chapter looks at some of the major ethical issues brought by technological and marketing changes for legacy news organizations that traditionally published static, physical-world news products. We include the issues raised in part by the case that opens this chapter—the new interactive relationships that news organizations have with news users and the eternal accessibility of news stories. Other ethical issues addressed in this chapter arise from legacy news media's need to cope with the loss of display advertising or broadcast commercials as their primary revenue base.

Here is a snapshot of some of the changes that legacy news media have needed to address in their move to digital publishing, compiled by media scholar Paul Grabowicz:

- In 2000, almost 50% of those polled read a daily newspaper; in 2010, that number was down to 31%. In 2002, the first year that this question was asked, 24% got their news online; in 2010, the number was 34%;
- With the advent of Craigslist and free classified advertising, classified ads have virtually disappeared from both virtual and physical news products;

- Governmental, corporate, and NGO web sites have user-friendly access and information, bypassing news media entirely when they want to deliver a crafted message to targeted audiences;
- While news organizations used to be very protective of their news products and copyright, "92 percent of [news organizations] polled in 2008 allowed readers to tag stories for inclusion on social bookmarking or aggregation sites (as compared with 7 percent in 2006)";
- Most news organizations have web-based reader comment sections that encourage readers to engage with one another in discussion of a story. Under the old paradigm, a limited number of column inches and words were allotted to a Letters to the Editor section;
- As of 2014, "some of the most popular news sites on the web were aggregators that pull together stories produced by a wide variety of other news organizations";
- "By 2008, 35 percent of adult Internet users had created a profile on a social network, as had 75 percent of Internet users 18–24. 72 percent of adult Internet users were using social networking sites like Facebook. The number in 2005 was only 8 percent";
- "About 47 percent of adult US Facebook users get news on Facebook, but a survey by the Reynolds Journalism Institute found that nearly 63 percent of people surveyed said they prefer news stories produced by professional journalists" (Grabowicz 2014).

The Reasons That Legacy News Media Endure

It might seem that professional news media are unnecessary in the digital era. Individuals produce and consume news through crowd-sourcing, amassing content on shared web sites and nudging framing choices through live or asynchronous conversation.

However, research indicates that users, including those who are digital natives, trust and believe legacy news organizations and dedicated online news sites over special interest information providers. "When people encounter information presented in a format that is associated with traditional media, they tend to evaluate the information positively" (Swasy, Tandoc, Bhandari, and Davis 2015, 227–228). The traditional journalistic values—verification, independence, and accountability—ideally are reflected in every news story published by any entity that claims to produce, aggregate, or share news. Legacy news media, along with a handful of digital native news sites, have credibility over other web-based information providers.

Media scholar Jane Singer says that shared values separate true news providers from other information givers. "[I]n an open environment that presents no limits on who can publish, journalists cite norms not only as identity markers of the professional news worker…but also as boundary markers between professionals and non-professionals…The distinctions they draw rest on ethical practices such as verification… principles such as independence…and promises such as accountability for the consequences of their actions" (Singer 2015, 21).

Verification, independence, and accountability are included in what Clifford Christians and other global media scholars have called universal values (https://en.wikipedia.org/wiki/Universal_value) or proto-norms (Caldwell 2014). These are conventions for reporting and publication that can be found across space, time, and culture. They are essential to the practice of producing news stories, regardless of who is publishing or where in the world the publication comes from.

Says Singer, "Although structural differences lead to variations in how journalists in democratic societies see their role, there are widespread commonalities in the articulation of fundamental professional norms. For example, the provision of reliable, factual information by impartial social watchdogs is seen almost universally as a central journalistic function" (Singer 2015, 22).

Verification serves as the "occupational boundary" for journalism. Web sites that operate with journalistic intent are those that are committed to providing balanced, accurate, relevant, and complete stories that fit the needs of their targeted audience members. The providers are committed to the principles of verification, independence, and accountability. "[J]ournalism calls for communication preceded by fact-finding and thoughtful consideration. Such approaches seek to reinforce the role of the journalist as authenticator, differentiating the profession from the work of others spreading similar information" (Hermida 2015, 43).

Although the majority of people find out about news first from family or friends or through social media contacts, users generally don't stop there. According to the Pew Research Center, "For nearly three-quarters of adults (72%), the most common way to get news from friends and family is by having someone talk to them—either in person or over the phone. And among that group, close to two-thirds (63%) somewhat or very often seek out a news story about that event or issue. Social networking is now a part of this process as well: 15% of U.S. adults get most of their news from friends and family this way, and the vast majority of them (77%) follow links to full news stories" (Mitchell 2013).

But the transition for legacy news organizations from the production of archival products, such as newspapers and broadcast news programs, to using the web as the primary platform for news delivery has not been smooth. News values have remained essential, but the nature of relationships that news organizations have had with citizens, content, and advertisers have needed to change.

Legacy News Media Adaptation to New Technology

Most legacy news organizations were early adopters of web-based technology, establishing a web presence in the early 2000s. "In 1996, only about 15 per cent of newspapers had an online presence. By 2009, most daily newspapers—even small ones—had websites" (Nielsen 2014, 472). But they brought traditional practices as well as traditional values to the new platform.

A review of 100 US online newspapers in 1998 showed that while 94 out of 100 newspapers reviewed provided at least one general e-mail address for users to contact newsrooms, fewer than one-third of those surveyed provided individual e-mail links for editors and reporters. At that time, only five of the newspapers offered a synchronous chat room. Only twenty-four conducted surveys or polls of their users. Only thirty-three ran discussion forums (Schultz 1999, 10–12). News managers clung to their twentieth-century habit of protecting story content for paid subscribers through paywalls, getting the word out first and producing unique framing for their narratives and pictures to compete with other news providers for audience members.

In early web publications, news organizations tried to stretch their traditional product to fit the contours of a new mode of presentation. Their early web site presentations were referred to by scholars as "shovelware (https://www.wordnik.com/words/shovelware)." Newspapers included the same content on web pages as they did in their print editions, sometimes formatting their websites so that the newspaper on the screen would appear just as it would in the printed physical copy. A study in the late 1990s "found that less than 10 percent of the 135 newspaper websites...studied offered any multimedia with news stories" (Weiss and Wulfemeyer 2014, 101). Historically, news media have first adapted new technology to traditional presentations rather than thinking about how new technology might create entirely new ways of presenting the news.

For example, journalism's first use of the new medium of live radio broadcast was equivalent to an audio book. Radio news in the early days was written in the same style as news produced for print publications but was read to listeners. Then, with the announcement of the World War II attack on Pearl Harbor, minutes after it happened, radio became the medium for breaking news reports. Radio announcers could report news immediately, which was a distinct advantage over the newspaper, which took time to print and distribute. Advances in portable audio recorders and transmitters allowed reporters to take the new medium out into the field when they went to report a story. Eventually, radio news broadcasts included natural sound and on-the-scene interviews with newsmakers and observers. At that point, it was clear that radio delivered a different kind of news from what was provided by print newspapers. As demonstrated by credible radio news providers around the world today, radio news found its niche in telling meaningful stories, incorporating a variety of voices, and using sound to invite listeners into the story's environment. While the conventions of news delivery were different for radio, the essential values of news transcended platforms.

Reframing Role-Related Responsibilities for Digital News

Once more, news organizations have been learning how to adapt to all that a new technology has to offer. By the early twenty-first century, legacy news organizations recognized the wisdom of thinking of news as web-based first, writing headlines with search engine optimization (https://en.wikipedia.org/wiki/Search_engine_optimization) in mind, and using multimedia and hyperlinks in telling the story.

News organizations began analyzing user input to better target their stories to their audiences. As one scholar explained, "Fox routinely tweaks the news on the Web to make the news more palatable to its audience. Even when it takes content from other sources like the Associated Press and puts it on its website, the organization tweaks the headlines to make them more attractive to its conservative audience. The AP's story 'Economic Worries Pose New Snags for Obama' turned into 'Obama Has a Big Problem with White Women'…Fox changes these headlines on the Web not because it has an agenda…but because people click on them more, meaning that more advertisements can be shown, and more money can be made" (Johnson 2012, 34).

In another example, Johnson explained, "The Huffington Post has turned content-creation on its head, using technology to figure out what it is that people want, and finding the fastest way to give it to them…. They employ a technology called multivariate testing to figure out what users want in near real time. According to Paul Berry, CTO, the site randomly displays one of two headlines for the same story for five minutes. After the elapsed time, the version with the most clicks wins and everybody sees that one" (Johnson 2012, 34–35).

Just as photography and radio technology changed the idea that news was something to be gathered, evaluated, and presented only in a narrative prose form, the web has added the real-time dimension to news as something that develops out of collaborative effort with users. In the new paradigm, news is immediate and interactive.

The interactivity between producer and user has created some editorial tension for legacy news organizations in prioritizing their goals for web-based production. One important goal, necessary to sustain credibility, is to provide news that is professionally gathered, mediated, and presented; these accounts must be balanced, accurate, relevant, and complete. Another important value, necessary to retain an online audience, is to sustain audience members who expect to be participatory in the virtual world.

Researchers have found that users are attracted to interactivity. According to media researcher Anders Olof Larsson, "A U.S. study indicated that users tended to feel a sense of commitment toward sites that offered more interactive features" (Larsson 2012, 255). Journalism in a digital era can be a partnership between news organization and user and a public discussion among citizens. As one visionary scholar noted in the 1990s, "The whole idea of the first amendment…was to empower people to use the news, not to make them dependent on government or a few journalists…New communication technologies have the potential of letting the public come closer than ever to realizing the full value of the First Amendment" (Himelboim and McCreery 2012, 404).

Ideally, the goals can be combined. "The mission to accurately and truthfully reflect society to itself remains a constant in journalistic ideology. However, how that mission is implemented and expressed is changing as the profession negotiates the tension between a claim to objectively parse reality and public participation in the news process…. Emerging practices indicate a shift toward verification as a collaborative, fluid and iterative online public process…The journalist moves beyond being the arbiter of 'the truth' and instead becomes a trusted professional who is transparent about how a news story comes together, with accounts and rumors contested, denied or verified in collaboration with the public" (Hermida 2015, 47).

For example, media scholar Jane Singer stated, "The fluidity of information on platforms such as Twitter means that material produced by journalists intermingles in myriad ways with material produced by users, bringing to the fore an emphasis on verification and transparency while lessening the importance of traditional norms such as objectivity" (Singer 2015, 29).

Some argue that interactivity should be discussed at the time a news organization decides to cover a particular story. Journalists should "include engagement elements in story pitches and budget lines" (Bullard 2015, 173). If how to engage users is embedded from the time that a story idea is launched, it is more likely that users will be invited to participate in the framing and development of the material.

How news organizations can best meet their role-related responsibilities using digital platforms is an ethical issue because it is important that news media do their job, regardless of platform. The importance of news media can be judged according to how effectively they help citizens actively govern themselves. One-way mass communication contributes to user passivity. Interactive communication encourages active participation.

Online Forum or Free-for-All

When legacy news media moved to digital platforms, most immediately opened up opportunities on the web sites for citizens to engage with one another as well as with the news organization. Many news organizations formatted their stories to allow for citizen discussion at the bottom of each. Reading a story online provided users with an easy view of what others had to say about the story and an opportunity to contribute as well.

Other news organizations opened up topic-specific discussions for stories that had great public significance. For example, within hours of the terrorist attacks on September 11, 2001, the *New York Times* opened a space for Internet users to discuss the events, attracting more than 2,000 comments within three days. "But while much of the content communicated a sense of shock and disbelief, some contained vitriolic, ethnocentric opinions that clearly would not be acceptable within the area of civil discourse" (Bressers 2003, 16). *NYT* staff responded by reviewing messages before making them public and deleting those deemed inappropriate. "No postings were allowed on the Sept. 11 board when moderators were unavailable and, for about two months, the board was closed at night and reopened in the morning. It was the first—and only—time a NYTimes.com board has had continuous oversight and restricted hours" but the online editor said that it could happen again (Bressers 2003, 17).

As with any public discussion, those contributing to online comments can be offensive and off-topic. They can also be civil, on-target, and astute in their observations. Generally speaking, journalists have said that they are not impressed with reader commenters.

In a study by media scholar Carolyn Nielsen, a journalist said, "[O]ur online commentators have little to offer anyone. They seem to be either morons or pranksters. I can't imagine any serious journalist worrying, or taking a cue from, an online post" (Nielsen 2014).

Some scholars and web editors have suggested that allowing anonymity on discussion sites leads to a lack of civility.

"The Reduced Social Cues model has shown how online users enjoyed a sense of equalized participation and status because their identities were concealed, protecting them from social judgments based [on] gender, age, race, class, etc. The other side of the model has been that individuals were depersonalized and the social norms that facilitate civility have disappeared" (Nielsen 2014, 473–474).

News organizations' response to uncivil behavior has been "to publish extensive codes of conduct for use of commenting spaces, in particular" (Singer 2015, 26). Other news organizations have accepted that they have responsibility for hosting (and policing) citizen commentary on their web sites as part of dialogical digital journalism. Doing so without censoring comments that might be unpopular with most users is a tricky balance for most online editors.

Some scholars have argued that allowing anonymity in user discussions is "a case of cognitive dissonance....The accepted standard of ethical conduct for the established media has been to review letters to the editor, op-eds and other third-party content for defamation prior to publication and to insist on printing authors' names. Newsroom codes of conduct tell reporters to avoid anonymous sources when possible and to use them only when the reporter knows the source's identity and has prior approval from an editor. Yet most online news organizations are willing to post, without editorial moderation, comments from faceless, pseudonym-tagged authors who could be writing from anywhere in cyberspace and to advance the agenda of any individual, organization, or corporation" (Hlavach and Freivogel 2011, 35).

Online reader discussions present a difference in kind from the printed editorial pages that include limited reader input chosen by editors. It is appropriate for news organizations to have different standards for different sections of their digital sites, just as they have different editorial standards in the publication of news stories as compared with the publication of comics or advice columns. User comment sections do not need to conform to traditional journalistic expectations because citizen commenters are not journalists. A reader comment section is like a public rally that has drawn together people with a common interest. Participation in public gatherings in which one expresses one's opinion verbally or simply by presence is not limited to those who identify themselves. One does not need to show an ID before holding a sign or slapping a sticker with a political slogan where it might be publicly viewed.

Credibility among people who are strangers to one another in the virtual and physical world develops based on what an individual has to offer. "[W]ithin the commenting sections themselves, some citizens carry influence as people cited each other, engaged with one another, and generally paid attention to the thrust of the conversation. They competed over 'facts' and tapped into the political and other power structures that have helped journalists attain the positions that they have. Citizens drew upon the linguistic ideologies of reporters to (re)name heroes and villains, create stories, and relate value systems. And they took on traditional journalistic roles such as historian to (re)articulate the meaning of significant events and crises and direct society on what lessons should be learned as well as on how to best move forward" (Robinson 2015, 162–163).

Rather than demand real-world identity for user commentary or review each comment for accuracy prior to publication, some news organizations actively moderate their sites. "Lindsay Howerton, who moderates the washingtonpost.com message boards, sees her role as a central force who bundles *Post* content for the online community and tries to stimulate informed discussion. She may question the accuracy of a posting, point out inconsistent logic, post comments intended to spur discussion and play devil's advocate" (Bressers 2003, 19). The involvement of a staff member may provide the interaction that users say they want in online environments as well as steer discussion toward civility. Engagement with citizens on the news organization's web site or on social media platforms has shown itself to be good for business.

According to Bullard, "One metropolitan newspaper cited hard evidence to demonstrate social media interaction pays off with increased readership and referrals to its website. Before naming a social media editor, whose role is largely to interact with readers, the newspaper had a consistent referral rate (readers coming to its website) of 13.4 percent to 14.8 percent from social media platforms. In the initial seven months with a social media editor, who also trained the entire newsroom on social media, social referrals ranged from 16.2 percent to 18.6 percent of its traffic. After adding a second social media editor and expanding its social media coverage hours, the paper's social media referrals ranged from 19.5 percent to 23.5 percent" (Bullard 2015, 180).

Other news organizations have resolved the issue of how to handle uncivility and reader comments by moving their comment sections to the organization's Facebook sites. This relieves news organizations of liability issues and the need to employ an editor to oversee commentary sections.

Corrections

When contacted by Levine in July 2015, the *New York Times* chose not to correct its 2007 profile of Pari Livermore. Executive editor Dean Baquet told Levine, "Unfortunately no newsroom in the country has the capacity to do 'background checks' on everyone it writes about."

Public editor Margaret Sullivan said, "The Times will be doing little else if it regularly adds notes to stories from many years ago in which there have been new developments, since each such note or correction requires some reporting and there would be something new to say about almost every story that has ever been published."

Standards editor Phil Corbett emailed Levine that he hadn't seen "any specific challenge to the facts in the Times story, which did not mention this particular charity," and he had no indication that "authorities were investigating or pursuing allegations of wrongdoing" (Buttry 2015a).

Media critic Steve Buttry took another position (https://stevebuttry.
wordpress.com/2015/08/28/is-there-a-statute-of-limitations-on-
correcting-errors-or-updating-flawed-stories/) and pointed out that
Levine had discovered, and Buttry had verified, that Spotlight on
Heroes was not registered as a charity at the time of the 2007 *Times*
publication. "The new development is exposure of a hole in the *Times'*
original story," said Buttry. In addition, Buttry pointed out that the
story was in error even if it didn't contain specific factual mistakes.
"Neither Levine's documentation nor *BuzzFeed's* reporting contra-
dicted the facts of the *Times* story, but they certainly contradict the
premise and exposed holes in the *Times'* original reporting. The *Times*
story didn't mention Spotlight on Heroes, but did describe the Red &
White ball as a 'charity event' in a year that the ball raised money for
Spotlight on Heroes" (Buttry 2015a).

Buttry argued that the profile merited correction because it was easily
accessible years later. "Levine read the *Times* story in considering paying
for Livermore's services, so eight years later the story was bolstering the
matchmaker's credibility as a legitimate charitable fund-raiser" (Buttry
2015a). When public editor Sullivan published a column addressing the
issue in November, Buttry wrote in his blog, "I think the *Times* should
have corrected the story, regardless of its age....While I disagree about
the need for a correction, I applaud Sullivan's acknowledgement that the
Times should have followed up on it when it learned about its flawed
premise" (Buttry 2015b). Sullivan's column had the important effect of
moving a *NYT* piece questioning Livermore's claim that Spotlight on
Heroes was a charity, up to the front page of a Google search on
Pari Livermore. A follow-up column by Steve Buttry includes (https://
stevebuttry.wordpress.com/2015/10/07/deni-elliott-journalists-often-
fail-to-think-beyond-charity-good/) an analysis of this case by one of
this book's authors.

Corrections made swiftly and as prominently as the errors they describe
are important to news organization credibility. According to one scholar,
"Corrections serve a dual purpose. They ensure that news consumers
receive the correct or updated facts, and they allow news organizations to
demonstrate their acknowledgement of a gaffe—showing that they are, in
other words, accountable for their mistakes" (Joseph 2011, 706–707).

Digital news corrections can take a form that leads to the complete disappearance of the mistake. Some news sites engage in what is called "error-scrubbing" or "stealth editing"—removal of erroneous text from the web site without notifying users of the changes. These organizations simply publish an updated version with the correct information inserted. Other news organizations correct substantial errors within the body of the article, with a note attached to the top or the bottom of the original explaining what changes were made and why. The corrections within the article may not be visible to the user. Yet other organizations red-line or cross out previous text so that readers can see where changes were made.

A 2010 review of national media corrections policies in the United States by MediaBugs.org revealed that corrections practices were "a mess." "We found that of the websites of 35 leading daily newspapers we examined, 25 provided no link to a corrections page or archive of current and past corrections on their websites' home pages and article pages. Only about half, 17 of the 35, provide a corrections policy of any kind... Sixty percent of the newspaper sites (21 of 35) do provide an explicit channel (e-mail, phone, or Web Form) for the public to report an error to the newsroom" (Follman and Rosenberg 2010). Silverman found that when citizens, or even investigating journalists, contact news organizations regarding errors, they are often ignored. "The other problem is that the news organization [*sic*] who offer an e-mail address, contact form, or other type of corrections reporting mechanism will often not respond or take action to requests from the public" (2010).

The lack of accountability for online publication is a problem for online news media throughout the world. Media scholar Justin Martin reported, "The websites of the *Economist, Foreign Policy,* the *Singapore Straits-Times,* the *Times of India, World Politics Review,* the *Moscow Times, Voice of America* and *Foreign Affairs* have neither visible corrections pages nor prominent corrections policies, to list a few" (Martin 2011).

A 2016 column by *New York Times* Public Editor Liz Spayd (http://www.nytimes.com/2016/09/25/public-editor/liz-spayd-new-york-times-public-editor.html) shows that progress has been slow in this arena. According to Spayd, "Times editors have thus far rejected appeals to flag readers when stories are reworked, unless it's a correction." She said, "When changes affect a story's overall tone or make earlier facts obsolete, or when added context recasts a story, readers should be told" (Spayd 2016). At the time of Spayd's column, the *New York Times* engaged in stealth editing, the *Washington Post's* policy was "to append an editor's note whenever substantial changes are made…[and] "BuzzFeed puts an update with explanation on any change that would affect how people might perceive a piece" (Spayd 2016).

Online corrections policies are difficult to find. None of the top ten online news entities named by Pew for 2015 had a direct and evident link from the home page to the organization's correction policy at the time that this manuscript was prepared for publication.

Implications of Immortal Stories

News organizations differentiate between their own choice to error-scrub factual mistakes and their policies on removing defamatory content in response to requests that the site "unpublish" stories in whole or in part. A survey of 110 editors from members of the Associated Press Managing Editors found that very few (20.9%) agreed that a news organization should unpublish a story because "The article contains outdated information that while accurate could be damaging to the source's reputation in the community," and only 10.4% of those surveyed agreed that a news organization should unpublish a story over "concerns that the post contains private information" (English 2009).

The reluctance of news organizations to unpublish true information is rooted in beliefs attached to static news products. Newspapers have traditionally published the so-called first draft of history. Each story served as an archival reference of some event of the day. Now, breaking news stories may evolve as new facts are learned, with new online versions published minutes apart.

When news organizations error-scrub, they illustrate an important difference in kind between static physical-world products and online publication. Unwillingness to ever unpublish stories at a story subject's request is contradictory to their own willingness to change online copy.

"One challenge raised by the changing practices of contemporary journalism is the need for news workers to determine whether or not a record of online news content should be maintained and archived in a way that mirrors print content. Journalists argued that while print content is typically viewed as a lasting record of history, the impermanence of online copy makes it easy for erroneous copy to be removed forever" (Joseph 2011, 712). If online publications are expected to be lasting records of history, then news organizations should entertain requests to unpublish.

This is an ethical issue because people are harmed by true stories that remain on the Internet eternally. "The permanent memory bank of the Web increasingly means there are no second chances—no opportunities to escape a scarlet letter in your digital past. Now the worst thing you've done is often the first thing everyone knows about you" (Rosen 2010). Even stories that are true might be held to have greater significance to the individual exposed than to any historical public record.

For example, in March 2014, the *Tampa Bay Times* needed to decide how to handle a case in which a local school board member "exploited his public office to inflate his teenage son's academic record in a scam involving take-at-home tests, altered grades and a bogus course description" (Tampa Bay Times 2014). There was no information in the news story or in the *Times*' editorial calling for the father's resignation to suggest that the teenager was an accomplice in his father's actions. Nevertheless, the teenager was named in the stories. A year and a half after the initial publications, these were the stories that popped up on a Google search on the now-young-adult's name.

While many North American-based and Australian-based news organizations have argued against unpublishing stories, the "Right to be Forgotten," decided by the European Union's Court of Justice in 2014, found that "Individuals have the right—under certain conditions—to ask search engines to remove links with personal information about them. This applies where information is inaccurate, inadequate, irrelevant or excessive for the purposes of data processing....At the same time, the Court explicitly clarified that the right to be forgotten is not absolute but will always need to be balanced against other fundamental rights, such as the freedom of expression and of the media. A case-by-case assessment is needed considering the type of information in question, its sensitivity for the individual's private life and the interest of the public in having access to that information" (European Commission 2014).

Ethical Issues Raised by Financial Changes

According to the Pew 2015 State of the News Media Report, "Newspaper ad revenue declined 4% year over year to $19.9 billion—less than half of what it was a decade ago" (Mitchell 2015). But although many social media and aggregator sites have reported significant revenue in advertising dollars, advertising has not supported legacy media on the web as it did when news organizations produced only physical-world products. "For all of these legacy news sectors, significant digital revenues remain largely on the wish list. None get more than a small share of their total revenue from digital, even though digital ad revenue across all media grew 18% in 2014 to $50.7 billion, according to eMarketer" (Mitchell 2015). Attempts to address the financial picture have included expanding advertising beyond traditional display and classified ads that are sponsored content, in-text advertising, and native advertising. News organizations are finding ways to entice readers who see their content elsewhere to click through to the news organization's web site. Other attempts include partnering with private interests or other journalistic organizations for special projects. Each carries ethical implications.

Incorporating Ads: Let Me Count the Ways

Advertising possibilities in digital formats seem infinite. Banner ads adorn news organization web sites. Advertisers can see that users have clicked-through to an ad and how long they have stayed once they arrived. Pop-up ads help drive clicks, even if the click that led users to the expanded advertising was actually intended to close rather than open the pop-up. Digital display advertising is annoying, but it becomes unethical if it is intentionally presented to mislead users into thinking that it is editorial copy.

Search engine ads pop up in response to user searches but are placed not by popularity, as are other search answers, but by payment. Paid ads in Google carry the notification "Ad" in yellow to indicate that the placement has been paid. Search engine users have learned to expect the paid ads but have different expectations for news sites. News organizations are reasonably expected to be independent in their news coverage.

In-text unit ads are the online text publishers' equivalent of product placement. In the entertainment world, cars, coffee, even breakfast cereal companies pay for their products to be placed in movies and television shows with the belief that users will buy products that they see used by celebrities or characters with whom they relate. Book publishers and online sellers, like Amazon, are happy to pay for hyperlinks that take users to their web site for easy purchase of books reviewed on news sites. The use of in-text unit ads has raised questions for news organizations about possible conflicts of interest. It is not clear to the users if books were chosen for review based on advertising or if the advertising followed the book review choice.

Native advertising refers to stories that are written by or for sponsors with the goal of creating copy that looks like news stories. "[N]ative advertising, or sponsored content, is a form of online advertising that is built around its resemblance to editorial content" (Coddington 2015, 75). But they are paid advertisements. While some news organizations slug such pieces as "Advertisement" or "Sponsored Copy" to make sure that users know that the content should not be confused with the news, native advertising sends mixed messages. The harder web sites work to make native advertising look like editorial copy, the less sense it makes to argue that calling something an "Advertisement" is going to make a difference. Users believe the visual—how something looks—over what is told to them in text. This is the type of digital advertising most likely to mislead users into thinking that the ad is news.

Project Partnerships and Creative Cost-Sharing

News organizations have also cut down on the cost of investigative or in-depth reporting by sharing those costs with a partner. Many times, the partnership is with another credible news organization. For example, a 2013 partnership that included the Center for Investigative Reporting, the *Tampa Bay Times,* and CNN resulted in a multifaceted story, America's Worst Charities, and won the prestigious Bartlett & Steele Gold Award for Investigative Business Journalism.

But partnerships with interested parties, even if the sponsors are non-profit organizations, can be suspect. In August 2015, the *Los Angeles Times* announced an initiative called Education Matters, "an ongoing, wide-ranging report card on K-12 education in Los Angeles, California and the nation" (Knefel 2015). Education Matters was funded with donations and grants from philanthropic organizations that include the Baxter Family Foundation and the Broad Foundation. The news organization can do little more than promise to do independent reporting in these circumstances. But the question remains if "independent reporting" includes critical review and reporting on funders. Whether journalists use their partners as sources or not, either approach seems destined to damage credibility or the depth of the story itself.

"Scholars and other observers have asked whether sufficient boundaries exist between journalists and their foundation benefactors in the nonprofit start-ups that have gained traction in the twenty-first century....Entrepreneurial journalism demands a reconsideration of the value (or not) of independence from audiences as well as advertisers or sponsors...In a traditional news environment, keeping audiences happy was only indirectly the job of journalists" (Singer 2015, 30–31).

Come for the Kittens; Stay for the News

Advertising revenue is determined, in large part, by the number of clicks to products news organizations can generate. As ads are displayed on web pages with editorial content, bringing readers to stories generates clicks to advertisers.

Clickbait can include stories with no or low news value that are there simply to draw viewers to the site. Clickbait can also refer to how elements of a story are presented. For example, a study of Danish news web sites showed that commercially owned news media used "forward-referring" clickable pronouns such as "he" and "this" at the beginning of online headlines, such as "<u>This</u> is an A-minus Paper," and "<u>He</u> loves Beatles," "as clickbait luring the readers into clicking on and reading the full article thus making the news site more attractive for advertisers" (Blom and Hansen 2015, 99). Clickbait becomes an ethical problem when story elements are stretched to sensationalize or draw in a user in a way that does not adequately reflect the story.

New Ethical Imperatives for Online News Sites

These guidelines are intended to encourage news organizations to use the power of digital formats while maintaining the essential principles of journalism.

1. *Encourage User Interaction*

The first step in developing a new interactive relationship with users is recognizing that the journalist's role has changed. According to media researchers Nee and Fusco, "This analysis shows that journalists had a role as distributor, aggregator and verifier of information, as well as facilitators of temporary communities online, through the use of hashtags, questions and re-tweets. The journalist also added value by crowd sourcing and keeping the conversation going" (Nee and Fusco 2015, 207).

Heather Chaplain, director of the New School's newly redesigned journalism curriculum, suggests that journalists and news organizations rethink their practice by focusing on "design as audience engagement." Chaplain says, "Designers always start by asking who they are designing for and why." From her perspective, that means starting with listening to the audience rather than the traditional beginning of crafting a story for publication. Says Chaplain, "You're out in the community that you're serving, saying, 'Hey, what do you need to know about, what are your information needs, and what's going on in your world that we can help you understand better?' It's not people sitting in a newsroom saying, 'These are the things people need to know'" (Ellis 2015, 3–4).

The key to user interactivity seems to be in educating journalists to think of their role in new ways. Along with verification and upholding traditional journalistic values to maintain credibility, media scholar Sue Bullock found that changing culture in the newsroom and educating reporters to embrace social media, as well as using a conversational tone and posing questions when posting to social media, drove more traffic to the industry web sites (Bullard 2015, 181).

2. Differentiate between Online and Static News Products

News organizations should determine news organization policy on online publication, demarcating the differences between online and static physical-world news products, and they should make that policy easily accessible.

If the organization's policy is that everything published, regardless of format, is considered archival, then nothing should ever be error-scrubbed or otherwise removed from an online story. If the publications are determined to be different in terms of what serves as the sustaining version, then a difference in unpublishing policy is also appropriate. Users should know the news site's policy.

3. Create Easily Accessible Corrections Policies

Attach corrections to stories, regardless of when errors come to the attention of the news organization or re-report the story with new information. Update quickly evolving stories with time-noted changes. If important statements of fact are changed, reference should be made to prior mistaken reports. Material should not vanish without explanation.

4.   *Clearly Differentiate between Advertising and Editorial Copy*

Advertising copy should never be allowed to have the same look and feel as news copy. News organizations should not produce or include advertising copy intended, by the advertisers, to fool readers into thinking that the ad copy is independently produced news and at the same time deny that readers are expected to mistake such ads as news.

5.   *Make Partnerships Transparent*

News organizations should be transparent with users about the agenda of any partner who provides sponsorship or expertise in the production of news. Sponsors should be transparent as well in articulating an understood boundary for their involvement in story production.

Questions for Reflection

1   Analyze codes of ethics intended for news sites in the digital era. How do they address the guidelines suggested here? What reasons might news organizations have for not addressing the guidelines suggested here?

2   Write a paragraph describing under what conditions news organizations should 'unpublish' a story or why they should never do so.

3   Search news sites for their online corrections policies. Count clicks, and look for other clues to determine accessibility to the corrections policy. How can users address "stealth editing"?

4   Search news sites for opportunities that they present for user interactivity. Find a news site that is interactive and find a site that is not. Which site do you find more appealing and why?

5   Choose an online news story as published on a legacy news site and determine ways that the news organization could better encourage user interactivity with the story.

Works Cited

Blom, J.N. and K.R. Hansen. 2015. "Click Bait: Forward-Reference as Lure In Online News Headlines." *Journal of Pragmatics* 76: 87–100.

Bressers, B. 2003. "What's Acceptable on Message Boards?" *Quill,* October: 16–19.

Bullard, S.B. 2015. "Editors Use Social Media Mostly to Post Story Links." *Newspaper Research Journal* 36 (2): 170–183.

Buttry, S. 2015a. "Is There a Statute of Limitation on Correcting Errors or Updating Flawed Stories?" The Buttry Diary, August 28. Accessed September 3, 2015. https//stevebuttry.files.wordpress.com/2015/08/times-livermore-story.jpg.

Buttry, S. 2015b. "New York Times Public Editor Notes Need to Update Matchmaker Story." The Buttry Diary, November 13. Accessed November 13, 2015. https://stevebuttry.wordpress.com/2015/11/13/new-york-times-public-editor-notes-need-to-update-matchmaker-story/.

Caldwell, M. 2014. "Proto-Norms and Global Media Ethics." *Communication* 40 (3): 239–252.

Coddington, M. 2015. "The Wall Becomes a Curtain, Revisiting Journalism's News-Business Boundary." In M. Carlson and S. C. Lewis, *Boundaries of Journalism.* New York, NY: Routledge.

Elliott, D. 1996. "Journalistic Research." *Journal of Accountability,* 4.

Ellis, J. 2015. "Building a J-School from Scratch: How The New School Aims to Bring Journalism and Design Together." Neiman Journalism Lab, August 31. Accessed September 1, 2015. http://www.niemanlab.org.

English, K. 2009. "The Longtail of News: To Unpublish or Not to Unpublish." *Associated Press Managing Editors,* October.

European Commission. 2014. Factsheet on the "Right to Be Forgotten" ruling. Accessed October 23, 2015. http://ec.europa.eu/justice/data-protection/files/factsheets/factsheet_data_protection_en.pdf.

Follman, M. and S. Rosenberg 2010. "The Wrong Stuff, Correction Practices at Major News Sites are a Mess, Survey Finds." MediaBugs November 8. Accessed October 23, 2015.

Grabowicz, P. 2014. "Tutorial: The Transition to Digital Journalism." Knight Digital Media Center Multimedia Training, September. Accessed January 4, 2015. http://multimedia.journalism.berkeley.edu/wp-content/uploads/2014/09/trans_digital_journalism-main.jpg.

Hermida, A. 2015. "Nothing but the Truth." In M. Carlson and S. C. Lewis, *Out of Bounds, Professionalism, Practices and Participation*. New York, NY: Routledge.

Himelboim, I. and S. McCreery 2012. "New Technology, Old Practices: Examining News Websites from a Professional Perspective." *Convergence* 18 (4): 427–444.

Hlavach, L. and W. Freivogel. 2011. *Ethical Implications of Anonymous Comments Posted to Online News Stories* 26: 21–37.

Johnson, C. A. 2012. *The Information Diet, A Case for Conscious Consumption*. Sebastopol, CA: O'Reilly Media, Inc.

Joseph, N. L. 2011. "Correcting the Record: The Impact of the Digital News Age on the Performance of Press Accountability." *Journalism Practice* 5 (6): 704–718.

Knefel, M. 2015. "LA Times' 'Independent' Education Project Bankrolled by Charter School Backers." FAIR, August 25. Accessed September 2, 2015. http://fair.org/home/la-times-independent-education-project-bankrolled-by-charter-school-backers.

Kovach, B. and T. Rosenstiel. 2007. *The Elements of Journalism*. New York, NY: Three Rivers Press.

Larsson, A. O. 2012. "Understanding Nonuse of Interactivity in Online Newspapers: Insights from Structuration Theory." *The Information Society* 28: 253–263.

Levine, N. 2007. Personal Correspondence.

Martin, J. 2011. "Apparently, Global News Orgs Don't Commit Online Errors." *Columbia Journalism Review*, July 27. Accessed October 23, 2015. http://www.cjr.org/index.php.

Mitchell, A. 2013. "State of News Media 2013." Pew Research Center.

Mitchell, A. 2015. "State of the News Media." Pew Research Center, April 29. Accessed September 8, 2015. http://www.journalism.org/files/2015/04/FINAL-STATE-OF-THE-NEWS-MEDIA1.pdf.

Nee, R.C. and J. Fusco. 2015. "Tweets During Crisis Follow One-Way Communication." *Newspaper Research Journal* 36 (2): 197–211.

Nielsen, C.E. 2014. "Coproduction or Cohabitation: Are Anonymous Online Comments on Newspaper Websites Shaping News Content?" *New Media & Society* 16 (3): 470–487.

Robinson, S. 2015. "Redrawing Borders from Within, Commenting on News Stories as Boundary Work." In M. Carlson and S. C. Lewis, *Boundaries of Journalism*. New York, NY: Routledge.

Rosen, J. 2010. "The Web Means the End of Forgetting." *New York Times,* July 21. Accessed July 25, 2010. http://www.nytimes.com/2010/07/25/magazine/25privacy-tw.html.

Rosenbloom, S. 2007. "Falling in Love for a Good Cause." *New York Times,* November 4. Accessed September 15, 2015. http://www.nytimes.com/2007/11/04/fashion/04match.html.

Schultz, T. 1999. "Interactive Options in Online Journalism: A Content Analysis of 100 U.S. Newspapers." *Journal of Computer-Mediated Communication* 5 (1): 1–19.

Silverman, C. 2010. "The State of Online Corrections." *Columbia Journalism Review,* November 10. Accessed October 23, 2015. http://www.cjr.org/index.php.

Silverman, C. 2013. "Washington Post Clarifies Practices and Standards for Corrections." Poynter.org, January 16. Accessed October 23, 2015.

Singer, J.B. 2015. "Out of Bounds, Professional Norms as Boundary Markers." In M. Carlson and S.C. Lewis, *Boundaries of Journalism, Professionalism, Practices and Participation.* New York, NY: Routledge.

Spayd, L. 2016. "Taking the Stealth Out of Editing." *New York Times,* September 25.

Sullivan, M. 2013. "Make No Mistake, but if You Do, Here's How to Correct It." *New York Times,* January 16.

Sullivan, M. 2015. "Pari Livermore, Nancy Levine and the New York Times: A Saga." *New York Times,* November 13. Accessed November 13, 2015. http://publiceditor.blogs.nytimes.com/2015/11/13/pari-livermore-nancy-levine-and-the-new-york-times-a-saga/.

Swasy, A., E. Tandoc, M. Bhandari, and R. Davis. 2015. "Traditional News Reporting More Credible than Citizen News." *Newspaper Research Journal,* 36 (2): 225–236.

Taggart, K. 2015. "Famous Matchmaker's Pet Charity Wasn't a Charity At All." *BuzzFeed,* July. Accessed September 15, 2015. http://www.buzzfeed.com/kendalltaggart/famous-silicon-valley-matchmakers-charity-is-oops-not-a-char#.ue48pDGvX.

Tampa Bay Times. 2014. "Get to Bottom of Rigged Grades." *Tampa Bay Times,* March 5. p. 8A.

Voice of America. n.d. "Terms of Use/Privacy Policy." Voice of America News and Information. Accessed October 23, 2015. http://www.voanews.com/info/terms_of_use_privacy_policy/1363.html.

Weiss, A. S. and T. Wulfemeyer. 2014. "Newspapers, TV News Offer More Online Innovation." *Newspaper Research Journal* 35 (2): 100–108.

3

Intellectual Property and Information Sharing

Is digitized information the right of anyone who reaches for it? Or is it a commodity, intellectual property (http://www.gnu.org/philosophy/not-ipr.en.html), to be bought and sold like clothes, cars, and other privately-owned items in the physical world? Are there new and better ways to think about the value of shared information in the digital era?

In this chapter, we will examine how the digital era, including news aggregation, has challenged traditional concepts of intellectual property and control. By the end of this chapter, users should understand different perspectives of how accessible information should be on the Internet and be able to identify differences between news aggregation and plagiarism.

Traditional copyright law (http://www.copyright.gov/circs/circ38a.pdf) and its advocates stand firm on the side of protecting ownership and profits, whether an individual's creation appears in the physical or virtual world. These advocates, and current law in most countries, prioritize the individual's right to earn revenue based on their creative output. Open-access activists argue that information available online should be free because it costs nothing to share digitized information; they also argue that some of the information kept behind paywalls, such as news items on some sites and research journal articles, is the kind of information needed most by those who can afford it least.

Ethics for a Digital Era, First Edition. Deni Elliott and Edward H. Spence.
© 2018 John Wiley & Sons Ltd. Published 2018 by John Wiley & Sons Ltd.

Sharing content, like so much of mass communication, is far easier in the digital era than when doing so depended on machines that made reduced-quality later-generation copies of printed text or taped audio or visual material. Everyone with access to the Internet can share information widely, as compared to the analog age when the owner of the original—referred to here as the originator—usually had the power to determine if and how it was shared. Differences between digital content and static physical world products have raised new conceptual questions: (1) Is there a difference between sharing and stealing? (2) What is the difference between news aggregation (https://en.wikipedia.org/wiki/News_aggregator) and plagiarism (http://www.plagiarism.org/plagiarism-101/what-is-plagiarism/)? (3) How has digitization affected how one can control one's original creations?

Copyright Law

Copyright law (https://en.wikipedia.org/wiki/Copyright_law_of_the_United_States) developed in the physical world originally to protect the rights of those who produced original material in the form of books, maps, and charts. It expanded to protect literary and artistic creations, including music and audio productions, paintings, and visual productions, such as photographs, films, and multimedia compilations. It now covers computer programs and databases, as well as three-dimensional art, such as sculpture. It restricts people who are not either the author or the owner of the copyright (which may be different individuals or organizations) from making copies or using the content without paying for the privilege or otherwise getting permission first. To make it even more complicated for a virtual global era, the length of copyright differs with different nations. Eventually, copyrighted work becomes public and cannot be restricted again. "Copyright law…protects only expression. Facts, ideas, systems, procedures, methods of operation, and many compilations of data are denied protection" (Menand 2014). Copyright protects architectural drawings but not copying of the building developed from those drawings. Copyright covers drawings and instructions on patterns for clothing but not the clothing itself. Buildings and clothing have what is called an intrinsic utilitarian function and are therefore exempt. And compilation of material, even if the compilation is creative, may or may not be protected. When a violation of copyright is found in the physical or virtual world, those using the content are legally required to cease using the content or explain why they are legally allowed to use the material.

Fair Use

The doctrine of fair use allows for limited free use of copyrighted material. This exception is meant to allow for nonprofit educational use, criticism, and news reporting or for the use of material, either in small amounts or the work as a whole, as the basis for creating new expression. Usually, scholars or students can make a single copy of an article or a book chapter for their own use, but they can't copy the whole book. They can quote from other sources and link to them in creating a new way of looking at a topic, as is illustrated in this book and in most other nonfiction works, but the vast majority of the content of the "new" work must be original. Another example of fair use is using copyrighted content as the basis for reporting the news. A new creation that satirizes the original piece counts as fair use, even if the whole original work is used.

Sampling (https://en.wikipedia.org/wiki/Sampling_(music)) uses small amounts from previously created musical compositions as overlays to create new compositions. How much original material can be used from previous compositions in sampling without violating copyright law has been decided by US courts on a case-by-case basis, with few clear guidelines for how to tell if the use of a particular use of a sample of a sound recording is fair use or a copyright violation. Australia, on the other hand, has issued more clear guidelines (http://www.artslaw.com.au/articles/entry/music-sampling/) based on the significance, rather than the quantity of material used. The rule of thumb is that if an artist wishes to use a sample from previous music because it will call to mind that original piece for listeners, then copyright permission is required.

Even the most obvious educational example of fair use can be complicated. For example, in the United States, it is a violation of copyright for a professor to make physical copies of an article to distribute to all students in a class. However, if the professor uploads each article to an electronic class site, each student is legally permitted to download one copy of each of the articles, print them out, and put them together in a binder for his or her own use.

Questions are also raised about just who really profits from copyright law and who is being asked to pay for the privilege of using material. "Academics... want access to the research in their fields. In the case of scientific research, much of that access is controlled by giant media companies like Springer, Elsevier, and Wiley. These companies publish academic journals and then charge huge subscription fees to the libraries of the universities that supported the very work they are selling back to them" (Menand 2014).

Copies in a Digital Age: Traditional Views and Open Access

Referring to digitized material as "a document" or multiple representations as "copies" is metaphorical at best. Instead of reduced-quality reproductions of original material that must be given away to be shared, multiple digital files can be created with no discernible difference between the original and any that follow. Each digital file is created anew. Everyone can have one without depriving another person of his or her own equally good rendition.

The *traditional copyright view* is that digitized material should be treated the same as intellectual property in the physical world. The usual analogy offered for this reasoning is that, just as most people wouldn't steal a car or a computer or wallet in the physical world even if someone left her house unlocked or her property unattended, individuals should not illegally take digitized material, such as downloading music, even if it is easy to do so. The analogy is that both acts are illegal. In addition, if the copyright owner has a legal right to be paid for use of her creation, then using the creation without paying deprives the copyright owner of revenue that is within her right to collect. The Digital Millennium Copyright Act (http://www.copyright.gov/reports/studies/dmca/dmca_executive.html), signed into law by President Bill Clinton in 1998, broadened copyright protection to include web-based material. This law was based on previous physical-world law and favored the originator in protecting the rights of owners to profit from "first sale." The act also protected Internet Service Providers (ISPs) from liability for third-party uploading of material that violated copyright law. ISPs are required to explain copyright protections to those uploading information to the site and to allow those who believe that their copyrights have been violated to post a "take-down notice (https://en.wikipedia.org/wiki/Notice_and_take_down)."

The **open-access view** is that digital copying does not deprive the original owner but rather creates more. Sharing, in this view, is not stealing. Open-access activists argue that multiple renditions do not necessarily deprive the creator of revenue. Artists do not get paid for their creations in the physical world unless others recognize the value of their work. Even in the physical world, an originator does not always get paid for use. A box full of books or CDs or software is worth no more than what others are willing to pay for those copies. Creating something does not automatically entitle the producer to compensation. Some online originators and aggregators request payment for what they offer, but they do not require it. Wikipedia, for example, has crowdsourcing campaigns (https://meta.wikimedia.org/wiki/Fundraising) that ask for contributions from those who use the service. This approach is not unique to digital communication. In the United States, National Public Radio and the Public Broadcasting Service have used pledge drives for decades to collect revenue from users; users voluntarily provide support for the services these entities offer.

Another online response to traditional copyright law is Creative Commons (http://creativecommons.org/about), which gives originators the ability to allow free use of their material but also allows them to protect it from commercial exploitation. This approach recognizes value to the originator but provides easier access for others, with the originator's permission.

Open access (https://en.wikipedia.org/wiki/Open_access) provides a more radical response in urging user and originator action to strip original content of licensing or copyright, moving content from the concept of individual rights to that of community resource.

Aaron Swartz, a software developer and open-access activist arrested in 2011 for using computers at the Massachusetts Institute of Technology to access scholarly papers kept behind a paywall, wrote in his Guerilla Open Access Manifesto (https://archive.org/details/ GuerillaOpenAccessManifesto), "[S]haring isn't immoral—it's a moral imperative. Only those blinded by greed would refuse to let a friend make a copy. Large corporations, of course, are blinded by greed. The laws under which they operate require it—their shareholders would revolt at anything less. And the politicians they have bought off back them, passing laws giving them the exclusive power to decide who can make copies" (Swartz 2008). Swartz killed himself in January 2013, before standing trial for his break-in at MIT. The *New York Times* reported at the time of Swartz's death, "While Mr. Swartz viewed his making copies of academic papers as an unadulterated good, spreading knowledge, the prosecutor compared Mr. Swartz's actions to using a crowbar to break in and steal someone's money under the mattress" (Cohen 2013).

As distribution knows no national borders in the digital era, copyright protection based on traditional nation-based point of origin (http://definitions.uslegal.com/p/point-of-origin/) law is increasingly difficult. There is no international copyright law (http://www.copyright. gov/fls/fl100.html). Whether use of particular material is fair use or is a violation of copyright or not depends on the country in which the material is distributed. Use of material in China, for example, cannot be prosecuted based on the US citizen-orginator's claim.

Some have suggested that protecting digitized material from being copied is a losing battle. According to Louis Menand, "According to an organization called Tru Optik (http://truoptik.com/), as many as ten billion files, including movies, television shows, and games, were downloaded in the second quarter of this year. Tru Optik estimated that approximately ninety-four per cent of those downloads were illegal" (Menand 2014, 84).

Some argue that what is most valuable in the digital era is not the static product but the ease of accessibility of that content and how much it is shared. Success in the digital age may be tied more to whether a creation goes viral (https://en.wikipedia.org/wiki/Viral) than to how much money the creation brings to the originator. According to an Australian scholar,

"The value of the digital 'asset' has shifted. No longer is value derived from the asset itself, since it is now infinitely duplicable. Rather it is found in the mechanism of access. Providing an efficient, convenient, reliable, fast, and reasonably priced mechanism for accessing content is vital for the longevity of creative business models" (Barkachi 2014, 24).

A final argument for open access in the digital era: it is easier than ever to see that all work is derivative (https://www.youtube.com/watch?v=jcvd5JZkUXY). If what is written or created today is based on what has come before, one might argue that no single person is solely responsible for seemingly new expression.

Aggregation and Plagiarism

Aggregation collects or points to information available from a variety of sources elsewhere on the Web. "News aggregation typically includes a hyperlinked headline, a citation to the original source and brief description of content. Most publisher web sites encourage link backs and canonical tags acknowledging them as original content generator. Linking drives traffic back to the original source and canonicals allow webmasters to prevent content duplication issues thus aiding in search engine optimization. News aggregators heavily rely upon fair use doctrine and driving traffic back to the original source" (Lakshika 2014).

On the surface, aggregation may look like a good thing for news sites, in that aggregators push traffic from the aggregation site to the news site, where entire stories and related material can be found. And, certainly, some users click through to original stories. But studies "found that 44 percent of Google News users scan the headlines without ever clicking through to the original articles on the newspapers' websites." Thus, "content originators are likely to argue that for many consumers, the use of their content by the news aggregators replaces the need for the original articles" (Isbell 2010).

Content originators argue that aggregators sometimes compete with them, using their original content rather than pushing users their way. Content originators claim that aggregators violate their copyrights by hot news misappropriation (http://scholarlycommons.law.northwestern.edu/cgi/viewcontent.cgi?article=1164&context=njtip). Material is more valuable when first produced. For example, an originator may object to an aggregator repeating when the originator is reporting minute-by-minute action at a sporting event, even if the aggregator includes the site from which information is originating. The originator may be happy with the final score to be shared (with credit) by the aggregator (Lakshika 2014). Originators would argue that, in this case, aggregator's use of information constitutes free riding (https://www.rcfp.org/browse-media-law-resources/news-media-law/news-media-and-law-summer-2012/content-aggregation-spreadi), as the aggregator is in direct competition with a product or service offered by the originator. Another type of free riding occurs when aggregators offer for free articles that originators keep behind paywalls and charge for their access.

Declining advertising revenue for legacy news sites and the uptick in advertising revenues for search engines and social media provide evidence that aggregators do compete with news sites for users.

Aggregators apply different techniques to compiling and publishing content and links.

Feed aggregators, such as Newblur.com (https://newsblur.com/), compile stories, including pictures and headlines, and post links to the originals. Framing is a technique used by feed aggregators to highlight information originated elsewhere.

Specialty aggregators collate collected information intended for individuals with particular interests, such as Topix.com (http://www.topix.com/) and Climatechange.org (http://climatechange.org/). Specialty aggregators exemplify the fair use exception in that they "contribute something new and socially useful by providing context and enabling comparisons between sources covering a story that would not otherwise be possible" (Isbell 2010).

User-generated aggregators use crowdsourcing to locate items of interest. YouTube.com (https://www.youtube.com/) and Pinterest.com (https://www.pinterest.com/) are popular examples of this type of aggregator. While users may upload original material, they often upload material found elsewhere, including that which is copyrighted. Sites such as these are required to notify users regarding what they can legally post and what they cannot, as Pinterest does in its Copyright Policy (https://about.pinterest.com/en/copyright). As ISPs are not legally held responsible for the copyright violations of third parties, all the ISP can do is agree to take the copyrighted material down when notified, which places the burden of keeping track of where material has been uploaded on the originator. In addition, Pinterest offers a "no pin" tag (https://help.pinterest.com/en/articles/prevent-pinning-your-site), which site owners can use to prevent Pinterest users from pinning content from their sites. However, it should be noted that the copyright policy is not easily accessible from the home page of either of these aggregators.

Blog aggregators rely on third-party content to create their blogs, linking to the original material after summarizing what is included. "In many cases, Blog Aggregators will have the strongest claim of a transformative use of the material because they often provide additional context or commentary alongside the material they use" (Isbell 2010).

Hybrid aggregators are examples of aggregators that use a combination of material. Facebook (https://www.facebook.com/) links back to news sites for examples, but also to Facebook friends' posts on the particular topic searched. Huffington Post (http://www.huffingtonpost.com/) includes original material, links to blogs, and reader commentary, as well as links to other web sites.

Whether aggregators are violating the copyright of the sites to which they link depends on where one draws the line between fact and expression. Facts are not protected. Expression is. Aggregators argue, for example, that headlines "do not qualify for copyright protection.... According to this argument, a headline is an uncopyrightable title or short phrase. Moreover, the argument goes, headlines are highly factual, and thus the merger doctrine would prohibit copyright protection. The merger doctrine denies protection to certain expressions of an idea (or set of facts) where the idea and its expression are so inseparable that prohibiting third parties from copying the expression would effectively grant the author protection of the underlying idea" (Isbell 2010).

The important conceptual difference between aggregation and plagiarism is that aggregators credit their sources. Plagiarists copy material and mislead the user into believing that they created the material rather than securing it elsewhere. Aggregated information should always credit the original source. Plagiarism is increasingly easy to identify, as search engines reveal online publications that have identical content.

Adapting Intellectual Property to the Digital Era

Some originators and aggregators have worked together to recognize intellectual property within digital communication. For example, some aggregators and originators have developed licensing agreements. These agreements respect original copyright while allowing for aggregating for a fee or with originator permission. "[A]rtists can create agreements that allow them to contract with multiple streaming services in order to gain as much revenue from as many services as possible" (Barkachi 2014, 25). In addition, originators have become more specific in stating how their work can be used. For example, the *Washington Post* (http://www.washingtonpost.com/wp-adv/archives/copyright.htm) policy reads, "You may not copy, reproduce, distribute, publish, display, perform, modify, create derivative works, transmit, or in any way exploit any content on washingtonpost.com, nor may you distribute any part of this content over any network, including a local area network, sell or offer it for sale, or use such content to construct any kind of database. However, you may download individual articles from washingtonpost.com for your own personal noncommercial use but only if you make only one machine readable copy and/or one print copy" (Washington Post 2002).

Open-access activists like Aaron Swartz choose civil disobedience (https://en.wikipedia.org/wiki/Civil_disobedience) to address what they think are illegitimate copyright restrictions. He said, "There is no justice in following unjust laws. It's time to come into the light and, in the grand tradition of civil disobedience, declare our opposition to this private theft of public culture. We need to take information, wherever it is stored, make our copies and share them with the world. We need to take stuff that's out of copyright and add it to the archive. We need to buy secret databases and put them on the Web. We need to download scientific journals and upload them to file sharing networks. We need to fight for Guerilla Open Access." Civil disobedience is ethical only if those who violate a bad law are willing to do so publicly and are willing to take the consequences that follow from their illegal activity.

Questions for Reflection

1   *Some cultures regard literary and artistic creations as community resources that should be free to all. Other cultures regard these creations as individual property that should be legally protected, like physical artistic creations.. Articulate the best arguments for each of these positions. Which do you favor? Why?*

2   *As journalists usually collect content from a variety of sources and then frame that information into narratives for user consumption, they might be considered the original "aggregators." How are ethical issues that legacy journalists face in crediting sources like and different from issues faced by aggregators that have developed in the digital era?*

3   *Find examples of the different types of aggregation (aside from the examples included in the chapter). Which of your examples are most likely to push stories back to the originator? Which are more likely to compete with the originator?*

4   *Find examples of identical stories published online that do not include credit to the originator. Look for ways to identify which came first.*

5   *Explore open-access arguments and look online for elements of civil disobedience. Describe some ways to determine the difference between civil disobedience and illegal downloading.*

Works Cited

Barkachi, P. 2014. "Copyright in the Internet Age." *Policy:* 21–26.

Cohen, Noam. 2013. "A Data Crusader, a Defendant and Now, a Cause." *New York Times,* January 13.

Isbell, K. 2010. "What's the Law around Aggregating News Online? A Harvard Law Report on the Risks and the Best Practice." Neiman Lab, September 10. AccessedJuly7,2014.http://www.niemanlab.org/2010/09/whats-the-law-around-aggregating-news-online-a-harvard-law-report-on-the-risks-and-the-best-practices/.

Lakshika, J. 2014. "News Aggregation: Fair Use, Legality and Way Forward." *Times of India*, September 11. Accessed November 15, 2015. http://timesofindia.indiatimes.com/india/News-aggregation-Fair-use-legality-and-way-forward/articleshow/42262106.cms.

Menand, L. 2014. "Crooner in Rights Spat: Are Copyright Laws too Strict?" *New Yorker*, October 24.

Swartz, A. 2008. "Guerilla Open Access Manifesto." Archive.org. Accessed November 27, 2015. https://archive.org/details/GuerillaOpenAccessManifesto.

Washington Post. 2002. "Copyright Information." *Washington Post* Archives. Accessed October 22, 2015. http://www.washingtonpost.com/wp-adv/archives/copyright.htm.

4

Citizen Responsibility in the Digital Era

College and graduate students can reach into every public offering of online pleasures and every hidden cave of secret knowledge and dark desires. The Internet is the time machine of the moment. We can travel past time zones, leap geographical distances, and eschew cultural taboos as we pop in to sample the world as others know it. We can place ourselves in the reality of recent past events or join the frontier of others' imagined futures. Virtual reality news apps allow individuals to put themselves in the middle of real-time circumstances.

As Arab Spring (https://en.wikipedia.org/wiki/Arab_Spring) and other uprisings in the early twenty-first century illustrated, the virtual world provides unprecedented opportunities for people to make change in the physical world. Citizens have the power to shape the world in their own view of what would make it better. They should do so. Citizens need to be engaged in creating the world in which they want to live because, according to political theorist Stephen Macedo, "Citizens deprived of the opportunity and the responsibility to grapple with the most significant moral questions lose a vital part of the training in responsibility and self-control that citizenship should bring" (Macedo 1999, 3). In the analog world, people could deny that they had any responsibility for events and issues outside their own backyards. Distance, disability, and time-lag

Ethics for a Digital Era, First Edition. Deni Elliott and Edward H. Spence.
© 2018 John Wiley & Sons Ltd. Published 2018 by John Wiley & Sons Ltd.

between events and reaction got in the way of most people becoming agents of change. Apathy was understandable.

Now there is no such excuse.

In this chapter, we share perspectives from philosophers Aristotle, John Stuart Mill (https://en.wikipedia.org/wiki/John_Stuart_Mill), and Albert Borgmann (https://en.wikipedia.org/wiki/Albert_Borgmann) in establishing the claim that individuals have role-related responsibilities to actively engage with other people and with society in a larger sense. Then we show how this responsibility relates to news media consumption. While only one of these philosophers wrote during the current communication revolution, citizens are better positioned now to fulfill the civic responsibilities described by all of these philosophers.

According to philosophers across the ages, citizens have the responsibility to take an active part in their communities for two reasons:

1. Citizens owe a debt to society for the protection and goods that they receive. The government that organizes the community provides common goods and protections for people who live within the government's control. Governments create and maintain laws that provide protection from those who would cause individuals unjustified harm and that hold transgressors accountable; governments provide relief in the face of natural disasters; some offer universal forms of health care.

2. Individuals cannot develop fully without testing out their ideas in the form of civil discussion with others. Engaging in civic life helps form and sustain good social habits and helps individuals figure out what they really think about important issues of the day. Engaging with others also allows individuals to identify, emulate, and ultimately become persons of good character.

How any particular individual chooses to get involved in civic life will differ based on the person's inclination and interest. But all adult citizens should, at least, cast votes in elections, which is legally required in some nations and voluntary in others. They should also add their voices in addressing issues outside of voting opportunities. Democracy thrives not on votes, but on the voices of citizens engaged in public discussion. Involvement may include volunteering in local community initiatives. It may include collaborating with other individuals and groups to address global issues such as climate change, world health, environmental degradation, or other issues that affect us all, regardless of where we live.

Digital mass communication allows for people to easily connect across time and space to share talents, skills, and perspectives so that they can come together to create change. Digital journalism helps individuals develop knowledge about the state of the world and how they can best engage in improving the world in which they live.

The Philosophers' Arguments

Aristotle

Aristotle was among the first philosophers to write about the responsibilities of individual citizens to engage in public life. He wrote most directly about these responsibilities in two of his works, *Politics* (http://classics.mit.edu/Aristotle/politics.html) and *Nicomachean Ethics* (http://classics.mit.edu/Aristotle/nicomachaen.html). In book III of Politics, written around 350 BCE, he focused his argument on building a healthy community. He wrote that what separated citizens from mere inhabitants of a geographical space is that citizens had the power to take part in government. He argued that, as every citizen has a stake in how government runs, salvation of the community is the common business of all citizens. He acknowledged that civil society predated any of the individuals he was addressing. Individual citizens did not ask to be born into a particular society, just as they didn't ask to be born into particular families, but they had obligations that followed from benefits received from where they found themselves to be.

Aristotle took a different tack in *Nicomachean Ethics*, where he discussed the moral growth and development of individuals. He argued that every person was biologically drawn to become as complete a person as possible. Growth is involuntary. It happens without individual choice. But just as it takes work to become one's best physical self, becoming a completely developed person, ethically speaking, does not happen without hard work. Development of moral imagination and ethical decision-making takes as much continuous exercise as the development of physical muscles and intellectual abilities.

Aristotle told us that people could not become their own best selves without the interaction that goes along with active citizenship (Peters 1893, 20). They needed to engage with those in our community because it is through connecting with others that people make the practice of virtue habitual. People learn how to be truthful by practicing being truthful. They exhibit honor by doing honorable acts. They learn not to be stingy or overly generous by having the opportunity to give to others and figuring out the right amount of personal philanthropy. They learn to be just by treating others justly. These virtues are dependent upon social interaction for enactment. Acting on those virtues embeds them within an individual's developing character (Peters 1893, 34).

In the world, individuals have an opportunity to watch people of "practical wisdom" in action. These are the people Aristotle said that citizens should emulate or go to for advice when they couldn't figure how to act in a tough situation. Seeking the wisdom of these people of good character helps others become people of good character.

In addition to interacting with strangers, Aristotle counseled that people needed true friends. Aristotle suggests that we are attracted to people who share our values. True friends, as differentiated from all sorts of other acquaintances, are those who help individuals become better people than they would otherwise be. They model virtue and hold their friends accountable when they fall short of being the best that they can be (Peters 1893, 227). Befriending a person who acts ethically tends to help individuals become more ethical.

John Stuart Mill

John Stuart Mill, a nineteenth-century British philosopher, focused even more sharply on the ethical responsibilities that individuals have to promote the good of the community. Mill provided two main reasons that individuals should engage in creating a better community:

First, like Aristotle, he argued that citizenship comes with responsibilities as well as with rights. In his essay *On Liberty* (http://www.

econlib.org/library/Mill/mlLbtyCover.html), in Chapter 2, Mill wrote that citizens have the duty to seek the truest opinions possible. He argued that the only way that anyone knows what he or she thinks is through testing those beliefs in discussion with those who think differently. In Chapter 4 of the same essay, he wrote that people have a duty not to interfere with the rights of others and to share in the work required to defend the nation and other citizens from injury.

Next, from his essay *Utilitarianism*, readers learn that individuals have the capability of being educated so that, through their own reasoning, they can see that their own happiness depends on the overall community being as healthy and happy as possible. For example, if an individual helps create and maintain shelters for people who are homeless, those in need are cared for. If homeless people are cared for, they are not forced to steal from others to get what they need to survive. They are not forced to live in unsanitary conditions that could create health problems for the community as a whole. Everyone benefits.

Mill wrote that personal fulfillment for the educated, enlightened individual was dependent on working hard to make the world a better place. Mill wrote, "[Y]et every man sufficiently intelligent and generous to bear a part, however small and unconspicuous in the endeavor, will draw a noble enjoyment from the contest itself, which he would not for any bribe in the form of selfish indulgence consent to be without" (Gray 2008, 146).

The more one engaged with others, the more perspectives that individual encounters. Mill wrote that most people "have never thrown themselves into the mental position of those who think differently from them, and consider what such persons may have to say; and consequently they do not, in any proper sense of the word, know the doctrine which they themselves profess" (Gray 2008, 42–43). If one believes that a woman has the right to choose to terminate her pregnancy, for example, it is not enough to know that others disagree with that belief. Mill said that proponents of one side need to put themselves in the mindset of their opponents to really understand their own beliefs. What is the reasoning behind one's own belief and the opponent's point of view? What is legitimate in the beliefs of advocates on both sides? What is not? Mill argued that an individual does not truly know what he or she believed without being able to answer those questions.

Mill taught that there are four reasons for seeking opinion different from one's own. First, the other opinion might be true. Second, it might be partly true. Third, even if the other opinion is completely false, understanding it helps the individual in understanding his or her own opinion better. Fourth, unquestioned beliefs become what Mill called "dead dogma." Beliefs that are held as dogma are those that everyone in a particular group considers to be community beyond question. Without questioning, beliefs develop into myths, conventionally held to be true regardless of any new knowledge or intervening facts.

Albert Borgmann (http://www.religion-online.org/showarticle.
asp?title=2901)

The last philosopher we'll invite in to this discussion is a contemporary philosopher of technology. Albert Borgmann taught that technology is a tool that can help or hinder individual development. Like Aristotle and Mill, Borgmann wrote of human fulfillment as relational, social, and active. But Borgmann studied how people achieve fulfillment amidst ever-changing technology He cautioned against letting techno-logical devices get in the way of people connecting with one another. Borgmann was even more concerned that, as devices become embedded and hidden, people would no longer notice when technology created a filter between them and others.

For example, consider shopping online as compared to shopping in a general store located in the center of a small town or in the neighbor-hood of a larger city. It is easier to click on one's computer to shop at Amazon.com than it is locate a few shopping bags and walk or drive to the town square.

When people do go to a physical store, they find that consumer choice among products is shaped by what is available in the store, the shop owner's access to distributors, the shop owner's choices of what to put on the shelves, and perhaps the season as well. Online sellers have a wider selection. On the other hand, online sellers present a purposeful hierarchy of items, sorted by crowd-preference or by what corporate sponsors have spent for good placement. Consumers usually do not think about why products are presented in the order that online sellers offer, as long as they can find what they need in a minimal amount of clicks. A few more clicks confirm the online purchase, which also hides the reality of the financial transaction. The cost will certainly appear on the user's credit card, but without the immediacy of a cash transaction. When people pay with cash in a physical store, they know immediately how much money remains in their wallet. One cannot overspend when relying on cash transactions.

Online shopping is possible without any connection to other human beings. Shopping at the local store is likely to provide individuals with information about the community, as neighbors greet one another: The school principal's daughter had her twins. The storekeeper got a new dog from that nice litter of Golden Retrievers born down the street. Blueberries are already ripe; harvest seems to be coming early this year.

Online shopping does not provide community-based information. It encourages others to buy another item or two, based on the algorithms computed from one's own previous buying behaviors or the behaviors of previous consumers. As was described in Chapter 1, shopping in the physical world for news provides the opportunity for accidental acquisition of knowledge not likely to happen in isolated online searching.

Borgmann echoed millennia of previous philosophers in arguing that individuals must have physical-world connections with others to become fulfilled human beings and to attain the good life. Fully understanding ourselves requires what Borgmann called focal practice: "A focal thing is something that has a commanding presence, engages your body and mind, and engages you with others....A focal practice results from committed engagement with the focal thing" (Wood 2003).

Musical instruments exemplify what Borgmann meant by focal practice. Playing a musical instrument requires engagement of body and mind. In addition, it connects the individual with a long historical "tradition of music and the community of musicians" over space, time, and culture. Technology distracts people from focal practice and engagement. It threatens individual and social growth. Choosing passive entertainment, like listening to music or watching television, takes up time that could be better spent making music with one's friends, telling stories or going for a walk.

Borgmann emphasized that social media friends are not a substitute for the real thing. Online relationships are derivative. The virtual interaction is dependent on an individual's beliefs about the person that lies behind the online persona. When individuals interact with online friends, they project beliefs about what the other is like in "real" life. More than one person has been disappointed to discover that the physical dating interest is much different from the online persona presented on the online dating site.

Digital Journalism, Audience Fragmentation, and Misperceptions

Online interaction is not sufficient for individuals to attain the good life (https://en.wikipedia.org/wiki/The_good_life). But ethical judgment is still necessary when citizens are seeking information online.

The first step is for individuals to think about their news media consumption. In the analog world, print and broadcast media gave the news to consumers. It was very difficult or impossible to get behind the news to analyze sources or context. However, as everyone in the community got the same news from a limited number of providers, information was commonly shared.

A world of views is available on the Web, but it is easy for citizens to consume information that does not take them out of their comfort zones. Users naturally gravitate to websites that provide short news pieces and frequent online spots that reinforce only what they already believe to be true. This causes audience segmentation (https://en.wikipedia.org/wiki/Audience_segmentation). Unlike the community sharing of information in the analog days, citizens choose news that seems right for them. News sites use data gathered from previous user navigation and then target stories and advertising that seem to fit the user's demographics. The more that users' personal views are reinforced, the more certain they are that they are right—and the less open they become to new ideas.

An example of how misperceptions can be reinforced by one's news source can be found in a study conducted by researchers at the University of Maryland in fall 2003, "Misperceptions, the Media and

the Iraq War (http://www.pipa.org/OnlineReports/Iraq/IraqMedia_
Oct03/IraqMedia_Oct03_rpt.pdf)." The American-led ground
offensive in Iraq ran officially from the invasion on March 20, 2003,
to May 1, 2003, when President George W. Bush delivered his
"Mission Accomplished" speech.

In this study, surveys conducted of more than 8,500 randomly chosen
Americans between January and September 2003 showed that more
than 60% of those polled had at least one of these three mistaken beliefs
about the War in Iraq:

1. Iraq (Saddam Hussein) was directly involved in the 9/11 terrorists
    attacks in the United States.
2. Weapons of mass destruction were found and/or Iraq used weapons
    of mass destruction during the March–May war.
3. World public opinion approved of the United States going to war
    with Iraq.

Researchers found a correlation between support for the war and
misperceptions. Twenty-three percent of those who had no misperceptions supported the war. Fifty-three percent of those who had one misperception supported the war. Seventy-eight percent of those who had
two misperceptions supported the way. Eighty-six of those who had
three misperceptions supported the war.

The poll also showed that where people got their news made a
difference. Eighty percent of those who got most of their news broadcast
or online from FOX news had one or more misperceptions. People who
got most of their news from NPR or PBS were least likely to have any
misperceptions, with only 23% of them having one or more. And, for
newshounds, who regularly used two or more news sources, including
at least one newspaper or news magazine, fewer than 30% had any of
these misperceptions (Kull 2003).

One way to know if one's favorite news source is providing the truth
is to use John Stuart Mill's test of checking out opinions different from
one's own—by seeing what other news sources, at various points on the
political spectrum, are saying as well. Disagreement over a vital fact
means that there is even more work for the critical citizen to do. Even if

the truth cannot be found, it is important to know the point of disagreement between news sources and why an important fact is in dispute. That can point the direction for how one might dig deeper to discover the truth.

Ethical News Consumption in a Digital Age

Media critic Dan Gillmor provided guidelines for how to best use news media for active citizenship. His paper "Principles for a New Media Literacy (https://cyber.law.harvard.edu/sites/cyber.law.harvard.edu/files/Principles%20for%20a%20New%20Media%20Literacy_MR.pdf)" started with the assumption that we are all producers and users of news. It is a choice of a few keystrokes as to whether one is consuming the news or creating a news product to be shared.

He preached the principles of skepticism, judgment, understanding, and reporting. These guidelines work both for news consumption and for news creation (Gillmor 2008).

1. Be skeptical and get out of your comfort zone. Check out controversial facts by reviewing how stories are reported by different news sites. Choose news sites that have credibility. Fairness & Accuracy in Reporting (http://fair.org/) (FAIR) and NetTop20.com (http://nettop20.com/) provide lists of news sites that include international sites and represent some prominent ideologies. But users should not be shy about exploring new and different news sites. The worst that could happen is having one's own true opinion reinforced by testing it out against other perspectives. Gillmor suggests seeking sites aimed at different target audiences, such as Global Voices (https://globalvoices.org/) and Black Planet (http://www.blackplanet.com/news/)for Euro-Americans. Qatar-based Al Jazeera America (http://america.aljazeera.com/?utm_source=aje&utm_medium=redirect) provides a Arabic-based source for important news coming from that region.

2. Ask more questions. Asking questions and listening to other perspectives, no matter how offensive those perspectives might be, helps individuals think of what it might be like to live differently or

hold radically different beliefs. Rather than challenging offensive beliefs, think of what it might be like to look at the world from that set of beliefs and think about how you could most honestly present the views of others.
3. In creating information for mass consumption, follow journalistic principles: Be right. Be fair. Be complete.

Information overload can be overwhelming. There are simply too many claims to research. Making the world better depends on active citizenship. Becoming an active citizen requires finding a cause and becoming a change agent.

Pseudonymous Engagement as a First Step

Media Scholar Clifford Christians summed up the responsibility for engagement this way: "The philosophical rationale for human action is reverence for life on earth, for the organic whole, for the physical realm in which human civilization is situated...technological products are legitimate if and only if they maintain cultural continuity" (Plaisance 2013). But individuals may hesitate to become involved if they fear reprisals for their actions. In addition, individuals may wish to be cautious when beginning engagement with virtual strangers. The development of a pseudonym for virtual civic activism can give users the opportunity to explore news sources and seek information about controversial issues without exposing their physical-world identities.

According to scholars Deanna Rohlinger and Jordan Brown, the anonymity associated with contribution to online political discussion "can buffer the risks associated with activism" because the Internet is not controlled by a single ideology or political group (Rohlinger and Brown 2009, 134). The bridge from pseudonymous virtual exploration to physical-world local activism is easy to construct. Physical-world community action is, in turn, sustained through digital communication and aggregation of relevant news topics.

Questions for Reflection

1 *Reflect on an experience that you have had in community engagement as an individual or, perhaps, through a school-based group assignment. What did you learn about your community that you didn't already know?*

2 *Identify a problem within your community or world that you would like to see improved. Is the problem better now than it was ten years ago? Is it worse? What groups are making the most progress?*

3 *Using a search engine, explore the different ways that your chosen community problem has been discussed. Separate out opinion pieces from those designed to inform. Are there factual disagreements between news sites and sources? Which ones are more credible and why?*

4 *Test your understanding of a different perspective on the chosen community problem by constructing an argument from the perspective that you don't hold. However wrong you might think that perspective, try to give it what Mill would call a fair hearing. Think about how you would help someone else understand your point of view.*

5 *Now, consider how you would like to make a difference in the world. How can digital communication help you connect with those who share your point of view or how can you engage in the physical world?*

Works Cited

Gillmor, D. 2008. "Principles for a New Media Literacy." *Media Re:Public.* Berkman Center for Internet and Society at Harvard University. Accessed November 20, 2015. https://cyber.law.harvard.edu/sites/cyber.law.harvard.edu/files/Principles%20for%20a%20New%20Media%20Literacy_MR.pdf.

Gray, J. 2008. *John Stuart Mill, On Liberty and Other Essays.* New York: Oxford University Press.

Kull, S. 2003. "Misperceptions, the Media and the Iraq War." WorldPublicOpinion. org. PIPA Knowledge Networks Poll, October 2. Accessed January 10, 2010. http://www.pipa.org/OnlineReports/Iraq/IraqMedia_Oct03/IraqMedia_ Oct03_rpt.pdf.

Macedo, S. 1999. *Deliberative Politics, Essays on Democracy and Disagreement.* New York: Oxford University Press.

Peters, R.L. 1893. "Aristotle, the Nicomachean Ethics." Online Library of Liberty, Inc. Liberty Fund. 1893. Accessed November 25, 2015. http://lf-oll. s3.amazonaws.com/titles/903/Aristotle_0328_EBk_v6.0.pdf.

Plaisance, P. 2013. "Virtue Ethics and Digital 'Flourishing.'" *Journal of Mass Media Ethics* 28 (2): 91–102.

Rohlinger, D. and J. Brown. 2009. "Democracy, Action and the Internet after 9/11." *American Behavioral Scientist* 56 (2): 172–188.

Wood, D. 2003. "Albert Borgmann on Taming Technology: An Interview." *The Christian Century,* August 23: 22–25.

Part II

Thinking Through Ethical Issues in Digital Journalism

5

DOIT, A Process for Normative Analysis

Beginning with the initial premise that the Internet has a global character, this chapter explains that a process for normative evaluation of digital information on the Internet necessitates an evaluative media model that is itself universal and global in character. The process has to be able to transcend cultural borders so as to be able to objectively evaluate the quality of information that is in its essence borderless and global. By cultural borders, we mean all types of borders, including geographical, national, ethnic, religious, gender, political, and lifestyle.

We use normative as a general term that collectively defines those epistemic principles that prescribe and guide what can be believed and known on the basis of justifiable evidence (epistemic norms) as well as those ethical principles that prescribe and guide ethical behavior (ethical norms). We provide, at the end of the chapter, a summary of the normative process for thinking through issues based on the ethically relevant aspects of digital journalism.

This chapter will show that information has a dual normative structure that commits all disseminators of information to both epistemological (those that relate to knowledge) and ethical norms (those that relate to moral behavior) that are in principle universal and thus global in application. Based on this dual normative characterization of information, the chapter will seek to demonstrate that: information and,

Ethics for a Digital Era, First Edition. Deni Elliott and Edward H. Spence.
© 2018 John Wiley & Sons Ltd. Published 2018 by John Wiley & Sons Ltd.

specifically, digital information on the Internet, as a process and product of communication, has an inherent normative structure that commits its producers, disseminators, communicators, and users, everyone in fact that deals with information, to certain mandatory epistemological and ethical commitments; and the negligent or purposeful abuse of information in violation of these commitments is also a violation of universal rights to freedom and well-being to which all agents are entitled by virtue of being agents (by agent we mean any person engaged in any purposive activity, such as taking a walk, searching the Internet, writing an essay, etc.,). We shall refer to the above argument as the Dual Obligation Information Theory (DOIT) (Spence 2009).

The primary objective of this chapter is to describe and propose a normative model for the theoretical and practical evaluation of the epistemic and ethical features of digital information on the Internet.

Any theoretical model for the critical evaluation of the cultural quality of information generally and of digital information specifically—particularly as it concerns the *creation, production, storage, search, communication, consumption,* and *multiple uses* of information both offline and online (collectively referred to as the *dissemination* of information)—has to be able to address the problem that there are many cultural varieties and differences, not always compatible or consistent, that exist both within and among nations. Cultural relativism, and more critically moral relativism, threatens from every corner. How does one propose—let alone provide—a theoretical (and practical) model for the evaluation of information that can address the problem of cultural and moral relativism?

Given the global reach and scope of the World Wide Web, which now reaches and affects every part of the planet, any theoretical model that seeks to not merely describe the cultural quality of digital information but *evaluate* it, at least in its epistemological and ethical manifestations, must itself be global in its application and scope. It must be able to evaluate digital information on the basis of universal principles that most if not all reasonable individuals, irrespective of their cultural differences and affiliations, can accept and, more importantly, must accept on the basis of their shared minimal rationality, which is necessary for all human communication. Communication cannot proceed let alone succeed if no one observed, for example, the rational principle of non-contradiction (that "A" and "not A" cannot both be true at the same time and in the same respect).

The abuse of information through, for example, misinformation practices, constitutes both a violation of the epistemological and ethical commitments to which the normative inherent structure of information, *as a process and product of communication* gives rise and a violation of universal rights to which all agents and specifically informational agents are entitled.

The Normative Structure of Information

The DOIT model is based on a minimal semantic definition of information: following Luciano Floridi, information is defined here as "well-formed meaningful data that is truthful" (Floridi 2005), and following Fred Dretske, information is further defined as an objective commodity capable of yielding knowledge" (Dretske 1999, 44–45; 86); knowledge in turn will be defined as "information-caused belief."

What is necessary for both information and knowledge is truth. Information without truth is not strictly speaking information but either misinformation (the unintentional dissemination of well-formed and meaningful false data) or disinformation (the intentional dissemination of false "information").

Of course, journalists cannot always *know* with certainty whether the information they disseminate is true. However, they should have a reasonable justified belief, responsive to at least some minimal objective verification capable of sustaining that belief, that the information they disseminate is probably, if not certainly, true. This consideration satisfies the absolute minimal condition of truthfulness. That is, disseminators of information with journalistic intent must at least ensure that to the best of their knowledge the information they are disseminating is probably true, if and when they are unable to know with certainty that it is true.

One could make the case, for example, that the dissemination of "information" by journalists concerning the claim that Iraq possessed weapons of mass destruction before the start of the war in Iraq was not based on a reasonable justified belief capable of yielding knowledge. Insofar as this was the case, the dissemination was misinformation at best, disinformation at worst. This was not a "reasonable justified belief" for journalists to hold because the evidence for the claim that Iraq had weapons of mass destruction was at best inconclusive. It was moreover uncorroborated by independent and credible sources. The information of those sources ultimately became known to be misinformation largely based on the overarching aim of the Pentagon of bringing about "regime change" in Iraq.

A central claim of this chapter is that all informational processes comprising the dissemination of information commit all rational agents to both epistemological and ethical conduct. Briefly, the argument is as follows: Insofar as information is capable of yielding knowledge—one must be able to learn from it—it must comply with the epistemological conditions of knowledge, specifically, that of truth or at least truthfulness. And insofar as the dissemination of information is based on the justified and rightful expectation among its disseminators and its users that such information should meet the minimal condition of truth or truthfulness, then the disseminators of information are committed to certain widely recognized and accepted epistemological criteria. Those epistemic criteria comprise the independence, reliability, accuracy, and trustworthiness of the *sources* that generate the information. In the example mentioned above, the sources for the information that Iraq had weapons of mass destruction were not credible because the sources of that information were largely not independent, reliable, or trustworthy. The epistemology of information in turn commits its disseminators to certain ethical principles and values, such as honesty, sincerity, truthfulness, trustworthiness, and reliability (also epistemological values), and fairness, including justice, which requires the equal distribution of the informational goods to all citizens. Thus in terms of its dissemination, information has an intrinsic normative structure that commits everyone involved in its creation, production, search, communication, and consumption to epistemological and ethical norms.

Information and Universal Rights

In addition to committing its disseminators to unavoidable epistemolog-ical and ethical standards, providing information with journalistic intent also commits its disseminators to respect for people's rights. News must not be disseminated in ways that violate people's fundamental rights to freedom and well-being (generic rights), individually or collectively, or undermine their capacity for self-fulfillment (negative rights). In addition, information must as far as possible be disseminated in ways that secure and promote people's generic rights and capacity for self-fulfillment (positive rights) when those rights cannot be secured or promoted by the individuals themselves and can be secured and promoted at no comparable cost to its disseminators (Gewirth1996; Spence 2006). But from where does this authority come, and what are the fundamental rights to which we refer? Alan Gewirth's Principle of Generic Consistency (PGC) offers a description and prescription for both the rational authority (based pri-marily on instrumental and deductive rationality) and the content of the fundamental rights (freedom = FR and well-being = WB) that persons have necessarily and only by virtue (sufficient reason) of being purposive agents.

Due to constraints of space, we will not attempt to provide a justifica-tion for Alan Gewirth's argument for the Principle of Generic Consistency (PGC) on which his derivation of rights is based, as this is well beyond the scope and limits of this chapter.[1] We will, however, offer a brief summary of the rationale of the argument for the PGC by way of a schematic outline of the three major steps of that argument.

The Rights of Agents: The Rationale for Alan Gewirth's Argument for the Principle of Generic Consistency[2]

Gewirth's main thesis is that every rational agent, in virtue of engaging in action, is logically committed to accept a supreme moral principle, the Principle of Generic Consistency. The basis of his thesis is that action has a normative structure, and because of this structure, every rational agent, by virtue of being an agent, is committed to certain necessary prudential and moral constraints.

Gewirth undertakes to prove his claim that every agent, *qua* agent, is committed to certain prudential and moral constraints by virtue of the normative structure of action in three main stages. First, he undertakes to show that by virtue of engaging in voluntary and purposive action, every agent makes certain implicitly evaluative judgments about the goodness of his purposes and hence about the necessary goodness of his freedom and well-being, which are the necessary conditions for the fulfillment of his purposes.

Second, he undertakes to show that by virtue of the necessary goodness which an agent attaches to his freedom and well-being, the agent implicitly claims that he has rights to these. At this stage of the argument, these rights being merely self-regarding, are only prudential rights.

Third, Gewirth undertakes to show that every agent must claim these rights by virtue of the sufficient reason that he is a prospective purposive agent (PPA) who has purposes that he wants to fulfill. Furthermore, every agent must accept that, since he has rights to his freedom and well-being for the sufficient reason that he is a PPA, he is logically committed, on pain of self-contradiction, to also accept the rational generalization that all PPAs have rights to freedom and well-being (Gewirth 1978, 48–128). At this third stage of the argument, these rights being not only self-regarding but also other-regarding, are now moral rights. The conclusion of Gewirth's argument for the PGC is in fact a generalized statement for the PGC, namely, that all PPAs have universal rights to their freedom and well-being.

Applying the PGC to information, we can now make the further argument that information generally and digital information specifically, must not be disseminated in ways that violate informational agents' rights to freedom and well-being, individually or collectively. Moreover, information must as far as possible be disseminated in ways that secure and promote the informational agents' rights to freedom and well-being. Conceived as the fourth estate and further identified to encompass the fifth estate, this places a significant and important responsibility on disseminators with journalistic intent.

For example, media release journalism (Simmons and Spence 2006, 167–181), in which some news sites misleadingly and deceptively present as objective and independently produced information that is actually given to them by public relations professionals, without disclosure that these so called "news stories" were produced to meet the needs of clients with private interests rather than the public interest. They are deceptive because they are designed to lead users to believe that the story was produced by journalists and written to promote public rather than special interests. Moreover, these practices constitute corruption, for they are conducive to the corruption of the informational processes and products that are essential for informing citizens on matters of public interest in an objective, truthful, and fair manner.[3] The topic of media corruption will be covered in Chapter 9 of this book.

Such practices, which once appeared only in the physical products of legacy news media, have become prevalent on the Internet, for example, in blogs that are purportedly produced with journalistic intent. Running media releases as though they were independently produced news items is demonstrably unethical on the basis of the PGC because it violates the rights to freedom and well-being that people have generally as agents and specifically, as citizens who require accurate, reliable, and trustworthy information on matters of public interest. If the deception involves collusion by PR professionals, journalists, and government representatives, in that they are all aware that they are intentionally misleading citizens, this violates all citizens' rights to freedom and well-being collectively by undermining the democratic process itself. Democracy requires truthful, fair, and objective production and dissemination of information on matters of public interest. It is partly for that reason that media control is sought and exercised by totalitarian regimes that do not want their citizens to be well informed.

In response to the claim that information must be true or at least truthful, and that intentional misinformation violates informational agents' rights to freedom and well-being, one could raise the objection that in some rare cases, deception might be conducive to the informational agents' freedom and well-being and thus be a justified exception. Investigative journalists sometimes use deceptive means to investigate, uncover, and expose government, corporate, or police corruption. This is justified if they have no other means of gathering data for matters of significant public interest, such as for example, government or police corruption, and if they are willing to explain to their audience members and the subjects of their investigation why they used these deceptive techniques. A successful argument will rest on their ability to show that deception was required to defend and promote the collective rights to freedom and well-being of all citizens to be informed on matters of public interest. A case in point was the 1970s *Washington Post* reporting on what is known as Watergate. There, some undercover deception by the *Washington Post* journalists was necessary in uncovering and exposing the Watergate political scandal that resulted in the uncovering of corruption in the US executive branch of government and the resignation of President Nixon. Matters of journalistic deception are addressed more broadly in Chapter 7.

The DOIT Model

Here is how to apply the DOIT model in thinking through ethical issues in digital journalism:

1. Does the information communicated meet the epistemic normative standards of truth or at least truthfulness?
2. Does the information provided meet the standards of independence and objectivity? For example, if the information provided is sourced from a PR press release on behalf of a client, then it should be identified as such and supplemented with independent and objective reporting and fact-checking before it is distributed as news.
3. Is the *source* of the information verifiable on the basis of reliable, trustworthy, and independent corroborative evidence? For example, does the source for the disseminated information on a scientific claim on climate change come from a credible and independent expert on climate change or from a news radio commentator with known sympathies and affiliations to those who deny climate change?

4. Is the evidence itself provided by the source of the disseminated information reliable and trustworthy?

5. In the case where the truth of the information communicated cannot be ascertained with certainty, determine whether its truthfulness can at least be established with a reasonable probability based on the disseminator's credibility, reliability, independence, and trustworthiness. As a general rule, the truth or truthfulness of the disseminated information is directly proportional to the reliability, independence, credibility, and trustworthiness of its source.

6. Finally, determine if the information disseminated supports or violates the rights to freedom and well-being of any agents, including story subjects, sources, or users. For example, as we shall see in Chapter 9, practices such as cash-for-comment or advertorials that masquerade as news stories violate the rights to freedom and well-being of their recipients, as they are likely to believe and act upon the information communicated.

Global Information Ethics: Cultural Relativism without Moral Relativism

In this section, we intend to expand upon an earlier claim by arguing that the DOIT model overcomes the problem of moral relativism while remaining responsive and sensitive to a varied and robust intra- and international cultural relativism that is undeniably present throughout the world. We shall argue that cultural relativism by no means necessitates or supports claims or calls to moral relativism. Moreover, cultural relativism even of the most varied and robust kind is theoretically at least consistent and compatible with the DOIT model.

This is at least for the following reasons. First, the kind of universalism that the DOIT model supports is neither ethnocentric nor dogmatic. The ethical universalism argued for in this chapter does not equate nor is it supportive of cultural homogeneity or uniformity. *Universality* is not the same as *uniformity*. The former, unlike the latter, is compatible with cultural variety and difference. It is a mistake to think that universality imposes uniformity. Insofar as the arguments adduced in this chapter in favor of both the inherent normativity of information, as a process and product of communication, and the universal rights to freedom and well-being to which it gives rise by virtue of the Principle of Generic Consistency are rationally sound and thus theoretically at least persuasive for all minimally rational agents, then they are universally applicable.

Let us first consider the inherent normativity of information per se, as a process and product of communication. That normativity, being inherent to information itself, cannot be affected by the contingencies of the variety and difference between cultures. For insofar as information as a process and product of communication must of logical necessity be true or truthful, the epistemological and ethical commitments to which that necessity gives rise are universally applicable to all informational agents, irrespective of their other legitimate cultural differences. Apart from some specific cases alluded to above with regard to investigative journalists, for example, misinformation by way of negligent or purposeful deception can never be justified, whether it takes place in the West or in the East. Interestingly but not unexpectedly, the notion of truth and/or its associated cognate concepts such as honesty, objectivity, and so on, features in most codes of media ethics across the world. According to the International Federation of Journalists, for example, *respect for truth and for the right of the public to truth is the first duty of the journalist (IFJ)*. Of course how and the degree by which people choose to *respond* to such deception from within their own particular cultural perspectives might vary from culture to culture. This, however, does not in any way diminish the ethical wrongness of misinformation. Good investigative journalism that seeks the truth, whether conducted in Russia, Africa, Asia, Europe, or the United States, transcends cultural and national borders. It is for that reason that in less democratic states, investigative journalists are both feared and persecuted, in some cases fatally.

In addition, since the universal rights to freedom and well-being of informational agents are based and derived from a rationally sound argument, namely, the argument to the Principle of Genetic Consistency, then they too are universally applicable. This universality is also conceptually consistent and practically compatible with cultural variety and difference. This is so because how people choose to interpret the degree of relevance of purposive freedom and well-being in their own lives, over and above the minimally necessary conditions for action, may undoubtedly vary from culture to culture with regard to specific cultural and social practices within those diverse cultures. That some minimal freedom and well-being is necessary for all purposive action remains, however, true and by logical consequence gives rise to universal rights. The *content* of those rights remains universal notwithstanding that the cultural *context* in which those rights are expressed, exercised, or withheld, may indeed vary from culture to culture.

One final point of clarification: It is not the intention of this chapter to convey that ubiquitous computing is the norm for all people across the globe. Far from it, the need for digital democracy to address the needs of those who do not have such access is addressed in our concluding chapter. The DOIT model, because it is universal, applies to all modes of information, analog as well as digital.

Questions for Reflection

1 *Why does the normative evaluation of digital information on the Internet necessitate an evaluative model that is universal and global in character?*

2 *What is information? Define its essential characteristics, without which it would not count as information.*

3 *What is misinformation and disinformation, and what makes them epistemically and ethically objectionable? That is, what is wrong about them?*

4 *What is the dual normative structure of information? Does it commit all disseminators of information and not just journalists to universal epistemological and ethical norms? What are the reasons for such a universal commitment?*

> 5   *What is epistemically and ethically wrong with media releases or press releases or any other communication of information in whatever format that masquerade as news or comment of journalistic intent without disclosure that the information provided is sourced from a media release?*
> 6   *Search and find recent cases of misinformation and disinformation and apply the analysis provided by the DOIT principle in this chapter to evaluate the ethical implications of those cases.*

Notes

1   For a detailed exposition and analysis of Gewirth's argument for the PGC, see Spence (2006).
2   A full and detailed defense of the argument for the PGC against all the major objections raised against it by various philosophers can be found in Spence (2006) Chapters 1–3; Beyleveld (1991); and Gewirth (1978).
3   For a further analysis and discussion of corruption generally, and media corruption specifically, see the following: Quinn and Spence (2007); Spence (2005); Miller, Roberts, and Spence (2005); and Spence and Van Heekeren (2005).

Works Cited

Beyleveld, D. 1991.*The Dialectical Necessity of Morality: An Analysis and Defense of Alan Gewirth's Argument to the Principle of Generic Consistency.* Chicago, IL: University of Chicago Press.
Dretske, F. 1999. *Knowledge and the Flow of Information.* Stanford, CA: CSLI Publications.
Floridi, L. 2005. "Is Semantic Information Meaningful Data?" *Philosophy and Phenomenological Research,* 70 (2): 351–370.
Gewirth, A. 1978. *Reason and Morality.* Chicago, IL: University of Chicago Press.
Gewirth, A. 1996. *The Community of Rights.* Chicago, IL: University of Chicago Press.

Gewirth, A. 1998. *Self-Fulfillment*. Princeton, NJ: Princeton University Press.

International Federation of Journalists. 1986. Declaration of Principles on the Conduct of Journalists. Accessed January 23, 2009. http://ethics.iit.edu/codes/coe/int.federation.journalists.html.

Miller, S., P. Roberts, and E. Spence. 2005. *Corruption and Anti-Corruption: An Applied Philosophical Approach*. Upper Saddle River, NJ: Pearson/Prentice Hall.

Quinn, A. and E. Spence. 2007. "Two Dimensions of Photo Manipulation: Correction and Corruption." *Australian Journal of Professional and Applied Ethics* 9(1): 44–60. Accessed April 5, 2017. https://philpapers.org/rec/QUITDO-9

Simmons, P. and E. Spence. 2006. "The Practice and Ethics of Media Release Journalism." *Australian Journalism Review* 28 (1): 167–181.

Spence, E. 2005. "Corruption in the Media." In Jeanette Kennett (ed.), *Proceedings of GovNet Annual Conference, Contemporary Issues in Governance*, Melbourne, Monash University: Australia.

Spence, E. 2006. *Ethics Within Reason: A Neo-Gewirthian Approach*. Lanham, MD: Lexington Books (a division of Rowman and Littlefield).

Spence, E. 2008. "Media Corruption." *International Journal of Applied Philosophy* 22(2):231–241.

Spence, E. 2009. "A Universal Model for the Normative Evaluation of Internet Information." *Ethics and Information Technology* 11 (4): 243–253.

Spence, E. 2010. "Information Ethics Without Metaphysics: A Neo-Gewirthian Approach." *International Journal of Technology and Human Interaction* 6 (1): 1–14.

Spence, E. 2010a. "The normative structure of information and its communication", *Journal of Information, Communication and Ethics in Society* 8 (2): 150–163.

Spence, E., A. Alexandra, A. Quinn, and A. Dunn. 2011. *Media, Markets and Morals*. Oxford: Wiley-Blackwell.

Spence, E. and B. Van Heekeren. 2005. *Advertising Ethics*. Upper Saddle River, NJ: Pearson/Prentice Hall.

6

Issues in Convergent Journalism

To borrow a term from Luciano Floridi (https://en.wikipedia.org/wiki/luciano_floridi), we now live in the infosphere. At last count, approximately 2 billion people worldwide (one-third of the world's population) used the Internet. Digital information can be created, accessed, disseminated, and used by anyone, anytime, anywhere—worldwide. This change challenges the traditional role and legitimacy of legacy news organizations as the primary and authoritative source of news. This is especially so on matters of public interest. The new world of citizen journalists ranges from the Twitterati (http://www.urbandictionary.com/define.php?term=twitterati) to the WikiLeaks (https://wikileaks.org/index.en.html) founder Julian Assange (https://en.wikipedia.org/wiki/julian_assange).

The primary aim of this chapter is to present a conceptual framework that shows how to examine and evaluate the ongoing transformations wrought by the digitalization of journalism and expansion of its communicators. Specifically, we will seek to show how this conceptual framework allows for the examination and evaluation of the ethics of the ongoing *convergence* of old and new media at the fundamental level of the *ethics of information*. We will show how this model can be operationalized to evaluate the impact of this convergence and its implications for the social well-being (*the good life*) of individuals and society. To that end, this chapter has three interrelated goals:

Ethics for a Digital Era, First Edition. Deni Elliott and Edward H. Spence.
© 2018 John Wiley & Sons Ltd. Published 2018 by John Wiley & Sons Ltd.

The *first* is to examine how the DOIT model, which was introduced in Chapter 5, can be applied simultaneously to digital and analog news media, so as to enable the identification and evaluation of the normative impact of their convergence. While contemporary news organizations focus on Web publication first, many retain production of static physical-world news products in print or through broadcast. Ethical expectations of news organizations apply to both virtual and physical-world behaviors.

The *second* goal is to examine how the use of DOIT can be applied to identify the *epistemological* impact (its impact on knowledge), the *ethical* impact (its impact on morality), and *eudaimonic* impact (its impact on well-being) of converged news media. Collectively, we will refer to the three separate impacts as the *normative impact*. This aim will be addressed in relation to two focal considerations: (a) in relation to the old media's traditional role of disseminating information to the public on matters of public interest and (b) in relation to the wider social implications and consequences that impact has on the well-being of individual citizens and society generally.

Finally, *the third goal* is to apply the normative model to some typical case studies to illustrate some of the types of epistemological, ethical, and eudaimonic issues that arise as a result of the convergence of old and new media.

The Fourth Estate

Traditionally, at least in Western democracies, legacy news organizations have been viewed, as the fourth estate: an important and essential organization for safeguarding basic rights of citizens, such as freedom of speech, and the right of citizens to be informed and heard on matters of public interest. Historically, the media and journalism in particular have exercised the role of protecting and promoting those basic rights. This has been done through the dissemination of essential information to the public that safeguarded those rights and the democratic system in which those rights have traditionally been in principle enshrined.

However, far-reaching technological advances in the digitalization of information and its global dissemination through the use of emerging information and communication technologies (ICTs) have profoundly and fundamentally changed the way in which information is now sourced and communicated. As the recent uprisings in Tunisia, Egypt, Libya, Bahrain, and Syria show, digital journalism, now available through the Internet, Twitter, smart phones, and social networks, such as Facebook and YouTube, are having a profound impact on the social life and democratic processes and practices of societies.

Beyond immediate political implications, digital news media also have the power to impact public life. The fundamental role of journalism as stipulated in its Australian code of ethics (MEAA (https://www.meaa.org/what-we-believe/media-regulation/)) (and echoed by its equivalents in the United States and elsewhere) is to disseminate information to the public on matters of public interest truthfully, reliably, fairly, and in a trustworthy manner, for the ultimate purpose of supporting and promoting a democratic way of life as an important and fundamental public good (at least in principle, if not always in practice). How has journalism in the virtual world changed that role? To answer that question we need to assess both the internal and external impacts. *Internally,* the impact is in the way that journalists use new media in sourcing and disseminating information through new media technologies, such as Twitter, for example; and *externally,* in the way nonprofessional communicators, such as bloggers, and new media networks, such as WikiLeaks, are disseminating information to the public.

Relatedly, since the dissemination of information can both benefit and harm us as individuals and collectively, as a society, we need to examine the wider implications and consequences of that impact on the quality of life of individual citizens and society. Is that impact good or bad in terms of how it affects our basic rights as citizens to freedom and well-being? For example, is the use of Twitter by journalists an appropriate technology for communicating a live-feed of court proceedings? Should jurors, who may see themselves as "citizen journalists," be allowed to access online information on defendants during a trial? Should they be allowed to "report" on the case after the fact? Is Julian Assange (https://en.wikipedia.org/wiki/Julian_Assange) a journalist, and if so, should he be allowed to disseminate information to the public in that role? If he is a journalist does he then have the right to the confidentiality of his sources and the protection of shield laws that protect all journalists? In order to answer those *practical* questions, we first need to ask the *theoretical* question how the impact of the convergence of new and old media can be reliably and objectively determined and normatively evaluated. Given the global reach of digital information through the affordance of the Internet and other ICTs, the importance of providing an answer to that question has both national and international implications.

The Convergence of Old and New Media: Five Paradigmatic Cases

Case Study 3.1: The Omnipresent Witness

The verbal abuse was recorded by a student of Athena Middle School on his mobile telephone and later posted to YouTube. The video shows Karen Huff Klein trying to ignore the verbal abuse to which she is being subjected, which included insults and threats.

The case of Karen Huff Klein (https://en.wikipedia.org/wiki/Bus_monitor_bullying_video) that was published and broadcast in the worldwide media, both offline and online, is a paradigmatic example of the convergence of new and old media. A digital media user videotaped a public event, which he then uploaded to YouTube; the video then went viral on the Internet; the story was then picked up and published worldwide as a news story that ran in virtual and physical-world publications. This is an illustrative case of what we describe in this chapter as media convergence—the convergence of digital media and corporate media in the dissemination of information to the public.

Case Study 3.2: The Wikileaker and NSA Leaker

Another recent case involving a whistle-blower is that of Chelsea (formerly Bradley) Manning (https://www.washingtonpost.com/world/national-security/judge-to-sentence-bradley-manning-today/2013/08/20/85bee184-09d0-11e3-b87c-476db8ac34cd_story.html), the twenty-four-year-old US Army intelligence analyst who stands accused of releasing the *Collateral Murder* (https://collateralmurder.wikileaks.org/) video as well as other classified documents to WikiLeaks.

The video shows unarmed civilians and two Reuters journalists being killed by a US Apache helicopter crew in Iraq. It received wide publicity in the mainstream media.

Another similar and more recent case is that of Edward Snowden (https://en.wikipedia.org/wiki/Edward_Snowden) who leaked highly sensitive information to the media about a secret government surveillance program, Prism, which he obtained while working as a contractor for the National Security Agency (NSA).

Both these cases demonstrate how news media in the virtual and physical worlds increasingly use content generated by digital media users and from media-activist sources, such as WikiLeaks and Edward Snowden, to inform the public on matters they consider to be of public interest.

Case Study 3.3: Fiction as Fact

The "Gay Girl in Damascus" (https://en.wikipedia.org/wiki/A_Gay_Girl_In_Damascus) case refers to an online blog, supposedly written by a young lesbian named Amina Arraf living in Damascus, that purported to give minute-by-minute reporting on the Syrian conflict. The blog was in fact a hoax that was written by Tom MacMaster, a graduate student from the University of Edinburgh. The photos of "Amina Arraf" proved to be those of a Croatian young woman living in the United Kingdom with no relation to Syria or the fictional "Amina Arraf." It attracted wide coverage from around the world, which led to its publication by the mainstream international media.

The application of DOIT to this case study clearly demonstrates the violation of both the epistemic and ethical responsibilities for disseminating information. First, the information, which turned out to be misinformation, was false, therefore violating the epistemic component of DOIT that requires the communication of information to be true or at least truthful. Second, the theft of the Croatian woman's digital identity and use of her photos to create the fictional character of Amina Arraf violated her rights to freedom and well-being. Publication also violated the rights of the many recipients of Tom MacMaster's misinformation, who were misled and deceived by his hoax, in violation of the ethical component of DOIT.

Whistle-blowers and leakers are traditionally seen as enemies by the holders of state secrets. Acting by stealth, as in Chelsea Manning's case, or openly, as in the case of Daniel Ellsberg (who leaked the Pentagon Papers, a secret dossier of documents on the conduct of the US political and military operations in Vietnam from 1945–1967, to the *New York Times* and other news organizations), they claim to act on moral conscience by undertaking to make public for the common good what the state wants concealed. Manning, Assange, and Ellsberg leaked information to the press that they believed that the public had a right to know.

Aligned closely to the public's right to information is the role of investigative journalists. Socrates, an ancient Greek philosopher from Athens (469–399 BCE), was probably the first investigative journalist. Socrates, just as his contemporary investigative journalists, sought diligently to uncover the truth. According to the Oracle of Delphi (http://ancient-greece.org/history/delphi.html) he was also the wisest. Being accused of "being irreverent to the gods and corrupting the youth of Athens," he told the court at his trial that like a "gadfly," his mission was to engage his fellow citizens in debate on matters of virtue, truth, and wisdom. He was sentenced to death by hemlock for his troubles. In his closing speech to the jurors, he reprimanded his fellow citizens for caring more about money and reputation than about morality and knowledge: "O my friend, why do you who are a citizen of the great and mighty and wise city of Athens, care so much about laying up the greatest amount of money and honour and reputation, and so little about wisdom and truth...Are you not ashamed of this?"(Plato (http://classics.mit.edu/plato/apology.html)).

Since Socrates, many good and worthy journalists have followed in those footsteps. These include the legendary US journalist Edward R. Murrow (https://en.wikipedia.org/wiki/Edward_R._Murrow), who took on Joseph McCarthy (https://www.google.com/webhp?sourceid=chrome-instant&ion=1&espv=2&ie=UTF-8#q=senator%2520joseph%2520mccarthy) in the 1950s and won at a time when all walked in fear of McCarthy; the respected Australian journalist Chris Masters, who exposed wholesale police corruption in Queensland in the 1980s; and two who, like Socrates, paid with their lives for informing the public of what they thought the public had a right to know: Irish journalist Veronica Guerin (1958–1996) and Russian journalist Anna Politkovskaya (1958–2006).

These journalists, whether consciously or not, shared Socrates's unshakeable conviction that truth and knowledge is the bloodline of a free democracy. And for present-day deliberative democracy, the dissemination of information to the public on matters of public interest is therefore seen to be essential. This provides some initial justification for the claim that the public has a right to know what the government is doing in its name.

Members of the public have that right in view of the fact that citizens are part of the democratic process and therefore must have the necessary information to enable them to participate, at least in principle if not always in practice, in the deliberations carried out on *their behalf* by their elected representatives.

That conviction is also expressed in Australia's *Media and Entertainment Arts Alliance* (MEAA) journalism code of ethics, which states that "respect for truth and the public's right to information are fundamental principles of journalism." Similar principles are also enunciated by the code of ethics of the International Federation of Journalists (IFJ), which declares that "respect for truth and for the right of the public to truth is the first duty of the journalist" (ifj.org (http://www.ifj.org/)).

Case 3.4: Techno-Media Corruption

The *News of the World phone-hacking scandal* (https://en.wikipedia.org/wiki/News_International_phone_hacking_scandal) has shown us that very bad things can happen when journalists aided by new information technologies turn from seeking truth to engaging secretly in crime and corruption, putting profit before propriety. Although the information sourced might have been true, it was not on a matter of public interest and was therefore not in the public interest to know. The information hacked by the *News of the World* was private information concerning various celebrities in the United Kingdom that might have been of interest to some readers of the *News of the World* for its gossip value, but it was not of public interest, as it did not concern matters that citizens needed to know in order to make informed decisions about issues that concern them as citizens, such as health, education, government, and so on. In addition, it violated the right to privacy of those citizens whose phones were hacked. Violating the legitimate privacy of citizens is not in the public interest if it does not promote some other overriding legitimate right, such as the right to national security, which was not the case in the News of the World scandal.

Case 3.5: Hackers and Hoaxers: The Online Activists

Related but different in its intention from the *News of the World* hacking scandal is the case of the self-confessed activist JonathanMoylan (http://www.smh.com.au/it-pro/the-hoax-we-had-to-have-20130110-2cix8.html#channel=f1d5abd2f00bca3&origin=http%253A%252F%252F www.smh.com.au). Moylan successfully perpetrated a hoax by issuing a fake media release claiming that the ANZ Bank of Australia had withdrawn its $1.2 billion loan from Whitehaven Coal mines, plunging the share value of that public company and disrupting the financial markets in Australia. Some applauded his action as constituting civil disobedience; others condemned it as a form of information corruption harmful to the public good. It divided public opinion across Australia.

Upon reflection, it is clear that Moylan's action was wrong according to the application of DOIT, as it was not true information but disinformation (a violation of the epistemic condition); moreover, it violated the legitimate rights of freedom and well-being of the ANZ Bank, whose corporate identity was misappropriated by being misrepresented through deception (a violation of the ethical condition). The rights of Whitehaven, as a legitimate corporate entity, which was the target of Moylan's hoax, as well as the rights of thousands of public investors in Whitehaven shares, who lost money when the value of their investment plummeted as a result of Moylan's deception, were also violated. Overall, Moylan's hoax was both epistemically and ethically wrong.

The New Journalists of the Fifth Estate?

In his article "Who is a Journalist," Jay Black wrote, "Broad-based citizen and web-based journalism augments the knowledge base and is making a persuasive case for enjoyment of the status, rights, and protections formerly enjoyed only by the elite media." He correctly points out, "Now is not the time to argue for a narrow definition of journalism" (Black 2010, 112).

He concludes that "the issue of who is a journalist should not center on where one works but on how one works" (Black 2010, 114). Black's wider definition of who is a journalist highlights correctly a major issue of journalism ethics raised by Christopher Meyers in the introduction to his edited book on that topic (Meyers 2010). Meyers argues that epistemic credence and trust is at the center of who and what a journalist is or at least ought to be in principle—not just in name and style but more fundamentally and crucially, in substance. We agree with both Black's wide definition of what constitutes a journalist and Myers's claim above concerning epistemic credence and trust. For what matters with regard to the dissemination of information both in the case where the dissemination is by a professional journalist of a major newspaper, such as the UK *Guardian* or the *New York Times,* for example, or by a "web-based journalist" or "citizen journalist" writing a blog on the Internet, is whether the information is credible and reliable with regard to truth and trust, especially on matters of public interest.

Insofar as Julian Assange, for example, has been disseminating information on his WikiLeaks web site that is true, credible, reliable, and trustworthy, and moreover information that is of public interest he can be, as he himself claims to be, a journalist—a journalist of the fifth estate. We define the fifth estate loosely here as the estate comprising all the world-denizens operating in cyberspace that, as individuals or groups, disseminate information on matters of public interest to the world at large and who are doing so with journalistic intent and who do so without fear or favor. They provide an invaluable service in the best tradition of investigative journalism but without the commercial constraints that unfortunately sometimes at least undermine, restrict, or even muzzle good investigative journalism, or worse still, lead to the kind of gross ethical and legal abuses evident in the News Corporation's *News of the World* phone-hacking case.

A symbiotic relationship has developed between the journalists of the legacy and digital media—and many journalists are both. Many journalists work for news organizations that produce physical-world products in addition to online news, and they likely produce content for digital and physical media simultaneously. When done correctly in accordance with the epistemic and ethical principles of DOIT, as in the case of the information leaked by Chelsea Manning on the *Collateral Murder* video and publicized by WikiLeaks and the mainstream media, that symbiotic relationship augments the quality and quantity of information disseminated to the public on matters of public interest and enhances the substance and scope of deliberative democracy. However, when false information or false sourcing is provided, as in the case of the *Gay Girl in Damascus,* the disinformation undermines the public interest and casts doubt on what one can accept as true or dismiss as false on the Internet. This is a major challenge to all journalists. Ultimately, it comes down to a question of trust in the truthfulness and reliability of the information.

Lee Wilkins correctly argues that in addition to their traditional role of informing the public, journalists should also seek to mitigate harm to the public. To do so, she says, the definition of news should not only include what actually happens but also what might happen. As Wilkins eloquently puts it, "preventing harm becomes the predominant ethical obligation" of journalists (2010, 313). Journalists, she argues, should become "mitigation watchdogs," anticipating and mitigating harm to the public. Wilkins's argument for "mitigation reporting" sits well with our own position that a global ethics requires not only a negative duty of not causing harm but also a positive duty of offering others positive assistance and promoting their welfare when we can (Spence 2007).

The argument that journalists should act as "mitigation watchdogs" adds further value and justification to the role that leakers and whistle-blowers, such as Chelsea Manning and Daniel Ellsberg, play in the worldwide dissemination of information to the public, with the helping hand of legacy-media journalists, as in the case of Daniel Ellsberg, and equally as citizen journalists such as Julian Assange, in the case of Chelsea Manning. The only thing we have to fear from true information that is of public interest is that its concealment by governments and the military can lead to far greater harm than its publication, specifically, when the information concealed is in the public interest and for the interest of supporting and promoting a healthy and robust deliberative and participatory democracy.

Questions for Reflection

1   *What do you understand by the term convergent media?*

2   *What is the difference between the Fourth Estate and the Fifth Estate? If there is a difference, what is the difference and does the difference matter in terms the quality of the news provided?*

3   *Are those who do not work for the legacy media but who use digital media to publish in the capacity of "citizen journalists" actually journalists? What is the difference, if any, between legacy journalists and "citizen" journalists? For example, although not a journalist was the person who recorded and disseminated the video in the Karen Klein case acting ethically in informing the public of an important matter of public interest?*

4   *Identify and analyze the main epistemic and ethical issues in the "Gay Girl in Damascus" case.*

5   *Identify and analyze the main epistemic and ethical issues in the Chelsea Manning Collateral Murder Case by seeking and finding further information on the case. Was Manning right in disseminating that information to the public via WikiLeaks? Was that information of public interest, and did the public need to know, despite the fact that the information leaked was classified?*

6   *Identify and analyze the main epistemic and ethical issues in the Edward Snowden case. Was Snowden right in disseminating that information to the public? Was that information of public interest, and did the public need to know, despite the fact that the information leaked was classified?*

7   *Does the Convergence between the 4th Estate and the 5th Estate make for better journalism in informing citizens on matters of public interest?*

Works Cited

Black, J. 2010. "Who Is a Journalist?" In C. Meyers (ed.), *Journalism Ethics: A Philosophical Approach*. New York, NY: Oxford University Press, 103–116.

Meyers, C., ed. 2010. *Journalism Ethics: A Philosophical Approach*. New York, NY: Oxford University Press.

Plato, *The Apology*. Accessed 16 May, 2012. http://classics.mit.edu/Plato/apology.html.

Spence, E. 2003. "Media Ethics: An Ethical Rationalist Approach." *Australian Journal of Professional and Applied Ethics* 5 (1): 35–44.

Spence, E. 2006. *Ethics Within Reason: A Neo-Gewithian Approach*. Lanham, MD: Lexington Books (a division of Rowman and Littlefield).

Spence, E. 2007. "Positive Rights and the Cosmopolitan Community: A Right-Centered Foundation for Global Ethics." *Journal of Global Ethics* 3(2): 179–200.

Spence, E. 2009. "A Universal Model for the Normative Evaluation of Internet Information." *Ethics and Information Technology* 11 (4): 243–253.

Spence, E. 2011. "Information, Knowledge and Wisdom: Groundwork for the Normative Evaluation of Digital Information and Its Relation to the Good Life." *Ethics and Information Technology* 13 (3): 261–275.

Spence, E. 2013. "Whitehaven Hoax Was an Unethical Act That Was Harmful to All." *The Conversation* 11 (January). Accessed 19 May, 2013. http://theconversation.com/whitehaven-hoax-was-an-unethical-act-that-was-harmful-to-all-11571.

Wilkins, L. 2010. "Mitigation Watchdogs: The Ethical Foundation for a Journalist's Role." In Christopher Meyers (ed.), *Journalism Ethics: A Philosophical Approach*. New York, NY: Oxford University Press, 311–324.

7

Privacy and Disclosure

George Bell, a seventy-two-year-old man, died from natural causes in his apartment in Queens, a borough of New York City, in July 2015. He had last been seen six days before his death. In the days before the body was discovered, a neighbor noticed that Bell's car had been ticketed for having been parked too long in the same spot. Bell didn't answer his phone. The neighbor noticed a "fetid odor" coming from the apartment and contacted the authorities (Kleinfield 2015).

The *New York Times* ran an 8,000-word front page story three months later that detailed Bell's life, from his childhood through his medical ailments, to the small apartment that was found filled with years-old trash. The story gave a detailed account of how investigators from the Queens County public administrator's office pieced together Bell's life and handled the governmental chores associated with the death of someone unknown to everyone around him.

Readers were told, and published pictures showed, that Bell had been a "hoarder (http://www.mayoclinic.org/diseases-conditions/hoarding-disorder/basics/definition/con-20031337)." His apartment was filled with decaying carry-out food containers, old newspapers, and worthless lottery tickets. Amid with the mess, investigators found "a half-dozen unopened ironing board covers, multiple packages of unused Christmas lights, four new tire-pressure gauges" (Kleinfield 2015), which they cited

Ethics for a Digital Era, First Edition. Deni Elliott and Edward H. Spence.
© 2018 John Wiley & Sons Ltd. Published 2018 by John Wiley & Sons Ltd.

as additional evidence that Bell suffered from hoarding, a mental illness characterized by a person's obsessive collection of unneeded items and failure to dispose of seemingly worthless items.

Bell's neighbors knew of no next-of-kin. He seemed to have no close friends. Eventually, investigators found a will that stipulated that Bell's assets should go to five people whom he had designated as heirs more than thirty years before his death.

Two of those people had since died.

The surviving three people were surprised to hear that Bell had left them money. He had never mentioned his will to any of them, including the one he had spoken to a few weeks before his death. The other two had not heard from him for years. None of them felt particularly close to Bell. None of them knew about his isolation or his hoarding.

The one person whom Bell had socialized with over the last fifteen years of his life, George Bertone, said that he didn't truly know Bell. Bertone said that they were drinking buddies and that they had spent some Saturdays together, fishing or talking. He had invited Bell to his home, but Bell, who never reciprocated with an invitation, declined to visit.

Bertone said that he didn't know that Bell was mentally ill. He said that "some eight years ago," he had stopped by Bell's apartment as he was passing by and that Bell had asked him to leave. According to the story, "A curtain draped inside the entryway had camouflaged the chaos." According to his neighbors, Bell had stayed "cloistered inside. Neighbors heard the regular parade of deliverymen who brought him his takeout meals" (Kleinfield 2015).

The George Bell story was read by "more than three million people in print, on the web site, or on their mobile devices," according to the *Times* public editor, Margaret Sullivan. As the behavior of digital users (http://www.reuters.com/article/idUSnGNX1nrLxR+1c5+GNW20141007) is tracked by news sites, *Times* editors knew that, "those who read it on their phones spent an average of six minutes on it—which, according to a newsroom memo, is 'an eternity in mobile-land'" (Sullivan 2015).

Many of the readers who commented on the story through the *Times* Facebook page were enthusiastic. They were touched by the compassionate tone of the story. They said that the story motivated them to reach out to isolated loved ones. But others thought that the news organization had violated George Bell's privacy.

"They wanted to know what gave the *Times* the right to splash a photo of his cluttered apartment over the front page for all to see, or to write about his old love letters, or his medical records." A reader said that as she read the story, "the more I felt uneasily like an intruder into a private life, understanding that the man in question had no say in what the world now knows about how he lived" (Sullivan 2015).

Public editor Sullivan devoted a Sunday column to exploring whether the *Times* story that lay bare the life and death of this private, mentally ill individual was justified. She decided that the publication was ethically permitted, even though Bell would probably have not given his permission for the story if he had been alive. Here are the reasons she gave:

1. Frank Bertone, who Sullivan called Bell's "best friend at the end of his life" and those that Bell named in the will were "excited by the idea and thought George would get a kick out of it";
2. There seemed to be no legal invasion of privacy as "a judge signed off on giving the paper access" to official records concerning Bell's death;
3. The executive editor, Dean Baquet, said, "I don't think the story had any true ethical issues…It doesn't hurt anyone and it's about a larger truth"; and
4. The *Times* made a decision that a greater good was served by thoroughly exploring Bell's life and death (Sullivan 2015).

At first glance, it seems odd that leadership at the *New York Times* took the time and space to address privacy concerns regarding their story about George Bell. But the story had been masterfully told by one of the best narrative journalists of the day. It engendered empathy among many readers along with comments from those troubled by the intrusion into Bell's life. Whether readers thought that the story was an important public service or one that had trampled the privacy rights of a fellow human being, they recognized that the isolation Bell experienced in the latter decades of his life might not be that unusual, with readers resolving to contact friends and relatives with whom they had lost touch. Readers also realized that they were as vulnerable as George Bell in having unflattering stories published about them after their deaths. They realized that professional and governmental entities that might be expected to keep information confidential after an individual's death failed to do so in this case. We will return to an analysis of this case at the end of the chapter.

Privacy and Confidentiality

Privacy (http://philosophytalk.org/community/blog/john-perry/2015/04/right-privacy) and confidentiality (https://en.wikipedia.org/wiki/Confidentiality) are interdependent concepts. In this chapter, we focus on the rights and responsibilities associated with privacy and confidentiality from the individual story subject's and individual news consumer's points of view. This chapter will focus on the individual's control over personal information and what is reasonable for individuals to expect from others who hold their secrets.

The chapter that follows looks at sourcing and story presentation through the lens of deception. Sometimes it is justified for journalists to withhold information from story sources, subjects, and users and sometimes it is not. Sometimes withholding information counts as deception. Sometimes it does not. The process of ethical analysis introduced in Chapter 5, DOIT, is used at the end of both this chapter and the next to illustrate how these concepts as they emerge in the practice of digital journalism can be judged ethical or not.

Privacy, most succinctly, is the legal or ethical right to be left alone. As we'll discuss it here, privacy includes the individual's ability to control the release of private facts and the individual's ability to live life without being stalked or otherwise being the subject of intrusion.

Confidentiality is the legal or ethical expectation that another person will protect information that the first individual wishes to be kept within the boundaries of that particular relationship. Some expectations of confidentiality are based on professional relationships such as those that clients have with doctors, lawyers, and accountants. The legal and ethical responsibility of these trusted professionals is to use that information, with client knowledge and consent, only to help their clients as best that they can. The information cannot be ethically used for any other purpose. But, confidentiality matters outside of professional relationships. For example, individuals who have close personal relationships with one another develop knowledge about the other that is expected to be held confidential. Even after a close relationship ends, it is reasonable for people to feel betrayed and cheated if confidential information is disclosed by previous partners. Entering into an intimate relationship conventionally carries the expectation that private facts will be held in confidence by the other even after the relationship ends. If this were not the case, no one could enter into an intimate relationship with the trust essential for that closeness.

Disclosure is voluntary sharing of specific information. Sharing information about others without their consent may be ethically problematic even if the facts themselves fall within the public realm.

The concepts of privacy, confidentiality, and disclosure make sense only within a social context. Privacy rights are not relevant if a person is entirely alone, cannot be monitored, and if information about him or her cannot be accessed by others. Confidentiality applies to information that one holds about another. Disclosure is relevant only if there is someone to tell.

The Shifting Boundaries of Privacy

Privacy rights can be violated many times over. According to philosopher Adam Moore, "If access is granted accidentally or otherwise, it does not follow that any subsequent use, manipulation, or sale of the good in question is justified" (2010). For example, an individual would have her privacy violated if she were secretly recorded while working alone at her computer in the privacy of her own home. If the person making the recording shared the content with his friends, that would be an additional invasion of privacy, causing additional harm. If the recording was loaded on YouTube and went viral, the violation grows exponentially.

Privacy is recognized as an individual "right," but how the concept is understood and protected is different among cultures. In the United

States, privacy is a civil right, with four legally recognized types of violations: intrusion, publication of private facts, presentation of an individual in a false light, and using an individual's person or identifying characteristics for commercial purposes without permission.

The *Universal Declaration of Human Rights* (http://www.un.org/en/universal-declaration-human-rights/), ratified by all fifty-eight member-nations of the United Nations in 1948, includes a broader understanding of the concept. It includes this description of the right to privacy in Article 12: "No one shall be subjected to arbitrary interference with his privacy, family, home or correspondence, nor to attacks upon his honour and reputation. Everyone has the right to the protection of the law against such interference or attacks" (United Nations 1948).

What counts as private information or as intrusion can vary among cultures and even within subcultures of a particular society. Whether an act is regarded as intrusion or comfortable familiarity depends on the circumstances and shared understandings of those involved. For example, knocking on doors and waiting to be granted permission to enter is one way that privacy is respected in some cultures. In other cultures, it is acceptable for people to walk unannounced through entranceways or to enter a friend's or family member's home without knocking. In some cultures, one rarely discloses one's ethnicity or religion; in others, requests for ethnic identification and religious affiliation are routinely made in the collection of demographic information. In yet other cultures, ethnicity or religion creates important social divisions, with individuals compelled to reveal that information.

Whatever the nuances of privacy in particular cultures, some shared understanding of privacy is important for people to function in social groupings and necessary for human development. According to Moore, "Controlling access to ourselves affords individuals the space to develop themselves as they see fit. Such control yields room to grow personally while maintaining autonomy over the course and direction of one's life" (Moore 2010, 17).

Technology changes how individuals and societies understand the concept of privacy. The fact that someone has a new ability to access information or to watch the actions of another does not justify doing so.

Rather, advances in technology require citizens and policy makers to consider how privacy protections should be expanded to cover techno-logical change. For example, when cameras first became available for commercial and private use in the mid-1800s, nations and citizens strug-gled over whether new laws should be enacted to protect individuals from being photographed without their permission. The reconsidera-tion of privacy brought about by this new technology re-affirmed a dis-tinction between private and public spaces. It was determined by most cultures that people automatically gave consent to being seen—and thus recorded—once they voluntarily stepped into the public arena. While some people might be uncomfortable with the proliferation of surveil-lance cameras in public, corporate, and governmental settings, citizens in most cultures have adjusted to the fact that giving up the right to be observed in these circumstances causes less harm for the community as a whole than failing to have surveillance. The Internet has piggybacked on the public/private distinction with the assumption that when people voluntarily log in to web sites through an Internet connection, they know that they are venturing into public territory.

In the pre-digital era, bits of information existed separately. Now, a simple Google search can compile a lifetime of information about a specific person. The Internet has created new cultural conventions regarding how and when people access others' information and what counts as consent for information about one's self to be shared.

Computers leave trails of previous connection, even when users choose not to reveal their physical-world identities. As users better understand the realities of digital exposure, particularly by those literally born to the Internet with their newborn pictures or even in-utero sono-grams published on social media, cultural privacy expectations may adapt. The expectations of those who seek digitally-based profiles may adapt as well, with potential employers less inclined to reject applicants based on what their Internet profiles imply. According to Moore, those who have grown up with digital technology are seemingly less concerned about controlling information about themselves than previous genera-tions, but in the early decades of the twenty-first century, there have been consequences for that lack of concern. "[T]hese individuals are willing to provide vast amounts of personal information on various social networking sites. Much of this information is mined and available to anyone who cares to look. For example, companies increasingly search for information about prospective employees that might indicate questionable past decisions or information that goes against the core values of the corporation" (Moore 2010, 175). It can be expected that nations will continue to develop regulations to protect individuals from the unlimited access and use of data that corporations had at the dawn of the Internet era.

A major difference between privacy in the physical world and privacy in the virtual world is that, in the physical world, individuals "opt-in (http://www.motive.co.nz/glossary/opt-in.php?ref)" for release of private information. If they stay in their homes and eschew communication of any sort with others, they literally can be "left alone." In the physical world, individuals have privacy unless they choose to open up access to themselves or their information. Sharing an intimate moment with another person or verbally sharing information with a confidant is likely to remain known to only those involved. They "opt in" to disclosing information about themselves.

In the virtual world, one's behavior is knowable, and one's information, though intended for limited distribution, is easily delivered to a world of others. As opposed to the "opt-in" principle that governs sharing of oneself and one's information in the physical world, the virtual world often operates on an "opt-out" principle. The default settings for users interacting on the Web is that users automatically receive newsletters, tips, and incentives to buy. Corporate interests make Internet connection and communication "free" for most users. The freedom to access many web sites and collections of information is provided to users in exchange for the site's ability to collect data concerning users' online behavior and content. The site owners/managers automatically have the ability to use what they know about an individual however they like. In some cases, users may "opt out" of certain levels of their information being used or shared. But the opt-out choice may not be easy to find, and updates by web sites may reset user choices back to a default setting that ignores previous privacy requests. News site managers are as eager to gather data about their users as managers of any other site. Data can be sold. It can be used to shape material. It most certainly is used to help advertisers reach their target audience members.

As the Internet matures, nations have begun regulating access and use of their citizens' information, once thought impossible due to the lack of "virtual borders." Some nations have begun to recognize individual privacy claims by requiring prominent notification of a site's range of information use and by requiring opt-in, rather than opt-out, policies. In addition, some nations have recognized that published or accessible information, even if true, may be harmful to the individual, with no justification of public need for its disclosure. "The EU Data Privacy Directives (http://ec.europa.eu/justice/data-protection/) define what counts as personal and sensitive information (name, address, health status, religious and philosophical beliefs, trade union membership, and sexual identity) and require that individuals be notified when such information is collected about them. Individuals further have the right to review and, if necessary, correct information collected about them" (Ess 2010, 55). The simple collection of data, even without disclosure, is seen as potentially harmful.

Technology has both created new challenges for those with pre-Internet expectations of privacy and has expanded the ability to shelter oneself from public view. Digital technology has also provided new ways that individuals can protect their privacy. Consider changes in how we talk on the phone with one another. In the old days of telephonic communication, one needed to answer the ringing telephone to find out who was calling. In the latter twentieth century, everyone living together often shared a single landline telephone number. When phones were first available, calls for an entire town were processed through a central human-operated switchboard or multiple households shared a single "party line" phone number. The identity of a caller, the time, and the duration of a call were all accessible by others. Switchboards, party lines, and even extension phones in the same residence made it possible, though not ethical, for others to listen in to others' phone conversations.

Now, with digital mobile devices, individuals are notified of the identity or phone number of most callers when the mobile signals the request for attention. The person receiving the call can choose to delay the call or not respond at all. Texting allows individuals to communicate privately, even in the full view and hearing of others. Unlike the pre-Internet days, when one had to physically turn away solicitors or sellers who came to one's physical door, ad blockers and privacy settings allow users to at least partially screen or block some corporate interests. Technology both creates new challenges for previous expectations of privacy and expands the ability to shelter oneself.

However, an individual's privacy rights do not legally extend beyond the death of that individual. George Bell was fair game for the *New York Times* because he had died. If he were a living reclusive individual, the equivalent story, exposing details of his life, written without his consent would have constituted a legal and ethical violation of his privacy.

Confidentiality

Confidentiality is the legal or ethical expectation that another person will protect information that the first individual wishes to keep within the boundaries of that particular relationship.

Physicians need access to a patient's medical information to order tests that the patient needs or call in a specialist on the patient's behalf. Lawyers and accountants need access to information about the amounts and locations of assets so that they can file taxes or deal with executing one's will upon death. Individuals may provide consent for those holding confidential records to share them with specific others, such as a primary physician sharing a patient's medical information with a specialist—but that sharing is done in the individual's interest, with the individual's consent, and with the expectation that all professionals in the chain will protect the individual's information. It is not ethically permitted for someone who has one type of confidential information to share it with another without the individual's consent, even if both professionals are acting on the same individual's behalf. For example, it is not ethically permitted for my physician to call my lawyer to let her know that I am not likely to live long and I should get my affairs in order. It is also not ethically permitted for my lawyer to call my doctor and let him know that I am really stressed out about not being able to pay my taxes.

Ethically, and in some nations, legally, the sharing of confidential information among professionals requires all three of the following:

1. Consent of the individual who has shared private information or consent from a surrogate decision-maker if the individual is unable to give consent;
2. Agreement that the information continue to be held confidential among those sharing it; and
3. That information be shared only on a need-to-know basis in the client's best interest.

Confidentiality is a necessary condition between partners in a life relationship and among friends. Friends and closest companions are reasonably expected to keep confidential not only what they have promised to keep confidential, but also any information that they have reason to believe that that the individual would want them to protect. In addition to private facts, the zone of information that one reasonably expects friends to keep confidential includes aspects of self that a close companion observes by being close with another in a series of life events over time. There is no law that requires such confidentiality, but it is an ethical requirement that supports true friendship.

Material held in confidence usually continues to be confidential after an individual has died. According to one scholar, "At an international level there is an agreement that medical data of deceased patients should continue to be treated as confidential and therefore be protected by law...After death, the physician is bound to confidentiality and if necessary should invoke his right to remain silent...Disclosure of medical data is justified when the agreement of the deceased can be presupposed, or (if this is impossible) if there are such important interests of third parties involved that the obligation to maintain confidentiality may be put aside" (Ploem 2001, 215).

The American Medical Association states "information contained within a deceased patient's medical record, including information entered postmortem, should be kept confidential to the greatest degree possible." The AMA provides a simple test: confidentiality protections after death should be equal to those in force during a patient's life. Thus if information about a patient may be ethically disclosed during life, it likewise may be disclosed after the patient has died (American Medical Association 2000). Otherwise, confidentiality should protect information even after death. Information may be ethically disclosed without an individual's approval in life or after death only if there is significant risk of harm to another, such as the transmission of a communicable disease, or if the person has made a credible threat of harm to him- or herself or to another. For example, a psychotherapist to whom a client has disclosed his intention to commit suicide prior to the detonation of a bomb he has previously set and hidden in a local school has the same ethical responsibility (and in many cases, legal responsibility) to alert authorities, whether the therapist reaches authorities prior to or after the client's suicide.

Other professionals, such as those in law, finance, and education, are also expected to keep client confidentiality during life and after death. Each profession has clear rules about when those expectations can be put aside. No profession allows disregard for client confidentiality simply based on a third party's perception that the overall community might benefit from the disclosure. If that were the case, no individual could trust that his or her information would ever really remain confidential, as it would depend on the fiduciary's subjective belief about the good of the community rather than the best interests of the client. The only ethical exception is when nondisclosure of confidential information puts others in direct and significant risk.

An Individual's Right to Nondisclosure

Digital communication has increased the opportunities for accidental disclosure of private information by individuals. Most people have had the experience of sending an e-mail to the wrong recipient or making a "butt call (https://en.wikipedia.org/wiki/Pocket_dialing)" on a mobile device. We consider ourselves lucky if embarrassment is the worst consequence of the mistake. Individuals are also vulnerable to accidental or intentional exposure by others. An offhand comment on social media may be meaningless to everyone—aside from the employer who believes that that disclosure shows an employee's disdain for company values.

An issue for individuals using news sites, or any Internet-based site, is whether they should be required to disclose their physical-world identities. While many news organizations initially provided space and encouragement for users to comment anonymously on their sites, by 2015, the tendency had swung away from allowing anonymity. According to journalists Kevin Wallsten and Melinda Tarsi, the "no anonymity" movement was motivated by two assumptions: "First when Internet users are allowed to post their thoughts anonymously, online discussions inevitably deteriorate into uncivil flame wars…Second, and more importantly, anonymous comments are assumed to exert a strong influence over Internet users" (Wallsten and Tarsi 2014). Pulitzer Prize-winning columnist Leonard Pitts wrote that anonymous comments sections encourage "bigotry, meanness, factual inaccuracy and plan nastiness" (Wallsten and Tarsi 2014).

Others have argued that anonymity encourages users to consider ideas rather than the person suggesting the idea, and thus, it allows for truly democratic discussions. In a virtual discussion with anonymity allowed, ideas may be separated from any prejudice participants might have regarding an agent's gender, sexual orientation, age, race, ethnicity, or disability.

Each of these views seems to be partly true. "The Reduced Social Cues model has shown how online users enjoyed a sense of equalized participation and status because their identities were concealed, protecting them from social judgments based [on] gender, age, race, class, etc. The other side of the model has been that individuals were depersonalized, and the social norms that facilitate civility have disappeared… While commenters are not sources in news stories, their comments appear on the same screen as the news articles and may seek to add details, correct inaccuracies in a news story, or add unverified or untrue information alongside the journalist's work" (Nielsen 2014, 473–474).

Just as with any discussion among people who don't know one another well, participants may be more open to hearing the views of others—or they may feel less accountable for causing harm to others through verbal abuse.

An argument against allowing anonymity for user commentary that seems flawed is the argument that news sites should not allow anonymous commenters because journalists are usually strong advocates for transparency and source identity. Media scholars Hlavach and Frievogel argued that allowing anonymity is "a case of cognitive dissonance...The accepted standard of ethical conduct for the established media has been to review letters to the editor, op-eds, and other third-party content for defamation prior to publication and to insist on printing authors' names. Newsroom codes of conduct tell reporters to avoid anonymous sources when possible and to use them only when the reporter knows the source's identity and has prior approval from an editor. Yet most online news organizations are willing to post, without editorial moderation, comments from faceless, pseudonym-tagged authors who could be writing from anywhere in cyberspace and to advance the agenda of any individual, organization, or corporation" (Hlavach and Freivogel 2011, 35). These authors suggest that the anonymous poster is "withholding part of the truth—his or her identity, a key piece of information that may help readers determine the author's credibility and motivation" (Hlavach and Freivogel 2011, 30). If the conversation is truly among private citizens, the likelihood of others who participate in the discussion knowing other random citizens well enough to judge or determine their credibility or motivations is unlikely in the physical world as well. Commenters earn credibility based on what they post. Those with credibility are those who are respectful of other views and who are transparent about their reasoning in reaching their conclusions. Commentary sections are different in kind from sections of the news product or production in which reporters or news managers exhibit control.

In the physical world, most people would object to a requirement that they wear ID badges as they move about in a public arena. When private citizens are asked for identification, the burden of justification is on the person requiring the proven identification of others, rather than on the individual who prefers not to offer identifying information about himself or herself. Adequate justification for demanding that people identify themselves is based on the need to protect the individual, community, or both. For example, it is justified for a law enforcement officer to ask for proof of identity, and for travel security agents at airports to ask for identification. It is also justified for banks and those handling other financial transactions to require proof of identity. But, individuals spend most of their time in the physical world unknown to others. We don't identify ourselves to strangers as we walk down the street. They have no need to know our identities. It is ethically permitted for a celebrity or a private individual to wear a hat and sunglasses when out in public. However, it is ethically prohibited for that person to act in criminal or uncivil ways while disguised.

One's physical identity is also not the business of electronic data collectors unless they have justification for requiring it. Data collectors' economic interests do not provide sufficient ethical justification for requiring disclosure of private citizens' real-life identities. The starting assumption should always be that people have the right to keep information about themselves private. Requiring the disclosure of one's physical-world identity silences the most vulnerable. Some individuals wish to keep their work life separate from their social life or want to engage with the community without the fear of consequences from employers or others whom they know in different aspects of their physical lives. Anonymous participation in virtual reality allows individuals to try on perspectives or explore issues in ways that they may not feel safe sharing with others.

Those who benefit from individual disclosure of physical-world identities on the Internet are primarily the corporations that have commercial interests in the data of individuals. That includes virtual news sites, which also have commercial interests. Those economic interests may play out in ways that are not in the best interest of users. According to one scholar, news organizations were found to be less likely to fight to protect the anonymity of those who comment on stories through their web sites than news story sources who requested that their identities be held confidential because comment pages were not of interest to advertisers. In fact, advertisers generally do not want their displays near inflammatory opinions. (Perez-Pena 2010).

News organizations have been experimenting with different ways of coping with anonymous comments; some have even made the choice to ban them altogether. Some news organizations place comments bearing the commenters' physical-world names higher in the comment queue; others require that commenters create an account within the news organization. These organizations keep the commenters' real names confidential from others in the public discussion, but commenters know that the news organizations can hold them accountable for any flames. However, by 2010, most news organizations changed their sites so that reader comments appear on Facebook rather than the news site itself, thus outsourcing both the ethical issues and the liability associated with unpopular opinions.

DOIT Analysis of the George Bell Publication

1. Does the information communicated meet the epistemic normative standards of truth or at least truthfulness? *The information about George Bell, his life, and his death was true or met the requirements of truthfulness.*
2. Does the information provided meet the standards of independence and objectivity? *The story was independently reported from an excellent and accomplished reporter from the highly credible* New York Times.
3. Is the *source* of the information verifiable on the basis of reliable, trustworthy, and independent corroborative evidence? *The sources of information on Bell's life and death were reliable and trustworthy and provided independent corroborative evidence.*
4. Is the evidence itself provided by the source of the disseminated information reliable and trustworthy? *There is no reason to doubt the truth of any factual claim made in the story.*
5. In the case where the truth of the information communicated cannot be ascertained with certainty, determine whether its

truthfulness can at least be established with a reasonable probability based on the disseminator's credibility, reliability,
independence, and trustworthiness. As a general rule, the truth or
truthfulness of the disseminated information is directly proportional to the reliability, independence, credibility, and trustworthiness of its source. *There is no reason to doubt the truth of any factual
claim made in the story.*

6.   Finally, determine if the information disseminated supports or
violates the rights to freedom and well-being of any agents, including
story subjects, sources, or users. *This is where the ethical issues arise.
As George Bell has died, one cannot argue that his freedom and well-
being are affected by publication of the story. However, the freedom
and well-being of sources and users certainly were affected by the
presentation of Bell's story. Living readers now know that private individuals ought not trust that confidentiality will be maintained after
their deaths. They have lost the freedom to believe that their private
facts will be buried with them.*

The decision of the *New York Times* to publish the George Bell story
illustrates how digital publication broadens exposure. In the pre-digital
age, if a private fact about an individual was published in a single
newspaper, the audience was limited to those who saw the physical
story. In a digital age, users access the story on computers and mobile
devices as well as in print. They click to share the story or a link to it.
Shortly after initial publication, stories may be picked up by aggregators
and by special interest online publishers. Memes inflate, exaggerate, or
satirize initially published content. Content goes viral.

In the *New York Times* publication, a worldwide audience of millions
of people learned details of this very private individual's life and death.
Now consider the reasons that public editor Sullivan offered as justification for publishing the material.

Sullivan said that Frank Bertone, whom she called Bell's "best friend
at the end of his life," along with those named in Bell's will were "excited
by the idea and thought George would get a kick out of it." But, according

to the published story, none of these people were aware of Bell's mental illness in the years toward the end of his life. It is therefore unlikely that any of them was an adequate judge of whether Bell would or would not have approved the story. Bell had not designated any of them as a substitute decision-maker for him. These acquaintances of Bell were not were given the *Times* story ahead of publication. Thus, they could not have provided knowledgeable permission for the *Times* to publish the story even if any of them had been in a position to provide surrogate consent.

Executive editor Baquet said that the story didn't hurt anyone. It is true that George Bell was not harmed by the publication; he was dead. However, part of what made readers uncomfortable about the story was the realization that they have no more power than Bell did to control what happens to them, their wishes, or their information after they die.

Baquet said that the story was "about a larger truth," and Sullivan echoed this perspective when she said, "a greater good was served by thoroughly exploring his life and death" (Sullivan 2015). This reasoning misuses the Utilitarian concept of greater good. The problem is that Baquet and Sullivan concentrated on harm caused to George Bell, rather than recognizing that the news organization caused harm to all who came in contact with that story. Dead people cannot be harmed, but living people may be harmed by the lack of trust that follows from knowing that private facts and information held confidential may not apply after their deaths.

Sullivan also said that there "seemed to be no legal invasion of privacy as 'a judge signed off on giving the paper access to the process'" (Sullivan 2015). While the reporter did not respond to e-mail from these authors that requested specific information about permissions requested by the newspaper and the judge's justification for granting it, it was likely that legal approval was needed for release of Bell's medical and post mortem information to the news organization. Bell's confidentiality was violated by those who should have held his information in trust; as Bell was dead, his privacy was not violated, but his confidentiality was.

This is where the *New York Times* story on George Bell failed to reach ethical justification. There is no reason to suppose that the deceased man dissected on the pages of the *New York Times* would have given his permission for the news organization to publish any and all material that a reporter could uncover about his life and death or that he would have given his permission for those who held confidential information about him to release it to the news organization. In conducting a harm-to-harm analysis, it is clear that members of the public would not have been harmed if the information regarding George Bell had been protected. It is also clear that we all were harmed by the exposure of George Bell.

Questions for Reflection

1 *How private are you? Read the "terms and conditions" and "privacy policy" of the two web sites where you spend most of your online time. What have you agreed can be done with information that you disclose and with details of your online behavior? Are you comfortable with this level of disclosure?*

2 *Is agreement to terms and conditions with which one disagrees voluntary or coercive? Explain.*

3 *Is it ethically permissible for professionals who hold confidential information about you to disclose it if they think that it will help the community better understand some issue? Why or why not?*

4 *What are some differences between being asked to give your phone number and postal code when you pay cash at a store in the physical world and being asked for such information when you sign up for an app in the virtual world?*

5 *What are some ways that you can create an anonymous Internet presence? What would you do as an anonymous wanderer in the virtual world?*

Works Cited

American Medical Association. 2000. "Opinion 5.051—Confidentiality of Medical Information Postmortem." American Medical Association. Accessed November 4, 2015. http://www.ama-assn.org/ama/pub/physician-resources/medical-ethics/code-medical-ethics/opinion5051.page?.

Ess, C. 2010. *Digital Media Ethics*. Cambridge: Polity Press.

Hlavach, L. and W. Freivogel. 2011. "Ethical Implications of Anonymous Comments Posted to Online News Stories." *Journal of Mass Media Ethics* 26 (1): 21–37.

Kleinfield, N.R. 2015. "The Lonely Death of George Bell." *New York Times*, October 17.

Moore, A.D. 2010. *Privacy Rights, Moral and Legal Foundations*. University Park, PA: Pennsylvania State University Press.

Nielsen, C.E. 2014. "Coproduction or Cohabitation: Are Anonymous Online Comments on Newspaper Websites Shaping News Content?" *New Media & Society* 16 (3): 470–487.

Perez-Pena, Richard. 2010. "News Sites Rethink Anonymous Online Comments." *New York Times*, April 11. Accessed November 5, 2015. http://www.nytimes.com/2010/04/12/technology/12comments.html?_r=0.

Ploem, C. 2001. "Medical Confidentiality after a Patient's Death, with Particular Reference to the Netherlands." *Medical Law* 20 (2): 215–220.

Sullivan, M. 2015. "A Private Man and His Very Public Death." *New York Times*, November 1.

United Nations. 1948. "Universal Declaration of Human Rights." United Nations. Accessed November 5, 2015. http://www.un.org/en/universal-declaration-human-rights/index.html.

Wallsten, K. and M. Tarsi. 2014. "It's Time to End Anonymous Comments Sections." *Washington Post*, August 19. Accessed November 5, 2015. https://www.washingtonpost.com/news/monkey-cage/wp/2014/08/19/its-time-to-end-anonymous-comments-sections/.

8

Deception in Sourcing and Presentation

Ethics commits everyone who claims to be publishing with journalistic intent to produce material that is as balanced, accurate, relevant and complete as possible. So, it may seem odd to use a whole chapter in an ethics book to discuss what counts as deception and under what conditions journalists' withholding of information in the process of gathering or presenting the news counts as deception. But deception is probably the ethics violation most often ignored or excused. People deny that they are acting deceptively when they withhold information that they have a duty to tell. "I didn't *say* anything false," is their claim. Others are quick to manufacture excuses for why it was okay for them to deceive *this* time and in *this* situation. Usually that excuse is that they were deceiving the bad guys.

In addition, new technology has multiplied the temptation to deceive as well as increasing the ability to escape detection. Technologically speaking, the Internet has given every one of us the equivalent of Harry Potter's invisibility cloak or the invisibility ring of Gyges (https://en.wikipedia.org/wiki/Ring_of_Gyges). Indeed, as we address at the very end of this chapter, one might reasonably conclude that the Internet has turned us all into liars.

Ethics for a Digital Era, First Edition. Deni Elliott and Edward H. Spence.
© 2018 John Wiley & Sons Ltd. Published 2018 by John Wiley & Sons Ltd.

The Nature of Deception and Its Justification

Deception is a behavioral choice. People act deceptively when they intentionally say something false or intentionally give a false message non-verbally, with the hope that the receiver of that message will come to a false conclusion. They also deceive when they intentionally withhold information (in some situations) with the intent of misleading others to a false conclusion.

Whether an agent has acted deceptively is based on the agent's intention, not whether the agent was successful. The act of *trying* to mislead someone to a false conclusion is ethically questionable, whether anyone has actually been misled or not. Once behavior has been accurately labeled as deception, the behavior requires further analysis. It is ethically prohibited to act deceptively unless one has justification that includes making a publicly-known rule that all others in the same situation would be equally justified in deceiving. For a more complete analysis, see (Elliott 1991 (http://digifolio.me/elliott/wp-content/uploads/sites/41/2012/05/On_Decieving_Ones_Sources1.pdf), 1992).

What Counts as Deception

If I say something that I know to be false, such as that I am a medical doctor when I am not, I have acted deceptively.

I have also acted deceptively if I say nothing at all, but I put on a white doctor's coat, drape a stethoscope around my shoulders, and stride with confidence through the hospital.

I have acted deceptively if someone stops me and says, "Hey, you are not a doctor," and I reply, "Yeah, right!" using sarcasm to mislead others into thinking just the opposite of what my words mean.

These are all examples of *active deception*. What is ethically relevant is that I have actively behaved in a way intended to lead one or more others to the false conclusion that I am a medical doctor. I have acted deceptively, even if my true identity as a journalist is discovered and I am thrown out of the hospital before I get to the celebrity patient's room where I hoped to get an exclusive interview.

Some deception is passive rather than active. One can act deceptively without saying or doing anything at all. Intentionally withholding truthful information is deceptive under any of the following conditions: withholding that information breaks the law; withholding the information is a neglect of duty or constitutes failure to meet role-related responsibilities; withholding the information breaks a promise; or withholding the information counts as cheating. Let's look at these in turn:

Intentionally withholding truthful information breaks the law if an agent is required by law to proactively provide certain information and he or she fails to do so. When filling out income tax forms, for example, citizens are required to disclose all income. If someone fails to disclose some of his income, he has acted deceptively.

In some countries, journalists are required to wear press identification when they are working. In other countries, journalists are required by law to disclose their professional identity when accessing nonpublic spaces, such as hospitals, homes, or private meetings. In some countries, such as the United States, journalists are not required by law to show any identification to legitimate their presence when working on a story.

Intentionally withholding information that violates one's duty or role-related responsibilities rests on the assumption that most legitimate societal roles require some proactive disclosure. A role-related responsibility associated with being a professor, for example, is that I give students truthful evaluations of their learning and progress. If I don't tell a student that he is performing poorly and let him continue to think that he is doing well in the class, I have acted deceptively, even if I say nothing at all to him. I am ethically required as a professor to let students know how they are doing.

Many professional ethics codes stipulate that journalists are required to disclose their identities. For example, the APN, a media company owning newspapers in Australia and New Zealand, expects the following from its employees: "We will clearly identify ourselves as journalists representing our news organisations at the beginning of any inquiry or interview, unless authorised by a senior editorial manager to do otherwise in the case of compelling public interest" (Australia/Oceania: APN News & Media: Editorial Code Of Ethics). The Canadian Association of

Journalists' Statement of Principles says, "Reporters will not conceal their identities, except in rare cases. When, on rare occasions, a reporter needs to go 'under cover' in the public interest, we will clearly explain the extent of the deception to the reader or listener or viewer" (Canadian Association of Journalists' Statement of Principles). Whether journalists are working for a legacy news organization or acting entrepreneurially, they should generally inform story subjects and sources of their role. If they violate this duty, in most cases, they have acted unethically.

Intentionally withholding information if that breaks a promise is also deceptive. If I co-own a boat with a friend and promise to get her agreement before loaning it out to anyone, I have acted deceptively if I fail to ask her before letting someone else use the boat. I have withheld information that I promised to disclose.

If a source likely to suffer harm through identification asks me not to identify her in the story, and I promise to let her know if my editor decides that we must name her in the story, I am required, by my promise, to tell her that she will be identified in the story. If I don't keep that promise, I have acted deceptively.

Intentionally withholding truthful information counts as cheating if I fail to follow the rules that everyone in a particular situation is reasonably expected to follow. If I don't disclose to my opponent that I have replaced a few of my Scrabble tiles when she was distracted by a phone call, I failed to follow rules that all Scrabble players in that situation are reasonably expected to follow. That's cheating. I withheld the truthful information that I made myself an exception to the rules of the game. In addition to having committed one unethical act—cheating—I have also deceived the other players by failing to disclose my act.

Journalists who do not tell a story subject that the article will present her in a negative way is withholding information in a way that counts as cheating. Many codes of ethics state an affirmative obligation to tell story subjects what is about to be reported about them. For example, the Australian Press Council Privacy Code includes the following, "[W] here individuals are singled out for criticism, the publication should ensure fairness and balance in the original article. Failing that, the media organisation should provide a reasonable and swift opportunity for a balancing response in the appropriate section of the publication" (Australian Press Council Privacy Code). The Alberta (Canada) Code of Ethics says, "It is the duty of newspapers to allow a fair opportunity for reply when reasonably called for."

Individuals and organizations should be given a fair and reasonable opportunity to reply to a personal attack or criticism (Alberta Code of Ethics). Reporters who do not give story subjects the opportunity to reply to negative descriptions that will be published are cheating. They are not playing by the rules that it is reasonable to expect journalists to follow in these situations. If they withhold this information from their sources, they are also acting deceptively.

Deception Is Ethically Prohibited Unless Justified

Some acts of deception are justified. Once an act is correctly labeled as deceptive, the next step is to consider if acting deceptively might be justified. As a starting assumption, truth-telling is presumed to be ethically permitted and deception is presumed to be ethically prohibited. An act of deception requires justification if it is to move into the ethically permitted realm. Deception may be justified by consent, convention, paternalism, or by harm vs. harm analysis.

Consent justifies an act that would otherwise be deceptive by negotiating a change in rules with all relevant parties. For example, journalists can deviate from normal expectations through agreement. If I am a story subject under attack, and a journalist tells me at the start of the conversation that he won't tell me the source of his information but that he will give me the opportunity to respond to the allegations made, I might talk to the journalist anyway. Without my agreement that he keep his source anonymous, the journalist would be withholding truthful information that he might otherwise have a duty to tell me. Not telling me would count as cheating. But if I agree for him not to tell me the source, but to share the allegations, then my consent provides justification for the journalist to withhold the name of the source.

Convention also provides justification for withholding information that would otherwise count as ethically prohibited deception. For example, the convention of reporting in the United States in public spaces is that journalists do not need to identify themselves. It is legitimate for a journalist to give her impression of a crowd's reaction or even to publish direct quotes that she overhears in public. In other countries, the conventions of reporting are different from this.

Paternalism as a justification for acts of deception means that that the temporary deception was intended to be in the best interest of the person being deceived. The classic example is that someone badly injured in a car accident may not be told that her companion died in the crash even if she asks. The interest in getting the injured person stabilized without the stress of knowing of the death justifies the deception. One can imagine news sites publishing emergency notifications for those in a particular area to leave immediately, due to imminent collapse of an earthen dam. If journalists withhold the speculation by some officials that everyone is not likely to make it out alive, this is justified deception because not publishing that information is likely to protect those attempting to escape. Publishing the information at the moment that officials are trying to get the community members to evacuate is likely to cause panic and increased fatalities.

Deception justified by *harm-to-harm analysis* includes acts where one can show that the harm caused by not acting deceptively is clearly worse than the harm caused by the deception. For example, many years ago, in the aftermath of a terrorist bombing at a US military base in Beirut, journalists from the *Wilmington (NC) Star* newspaper launched their own pseudo-terrorist attack at the nearby Camp Lejeune marine base. Complaints about lack of security on the base were longstanding. Military leadership insisted that the base was secure and well-protected. The only way that journalists could test out the truth of that assertion was to check it out themselves. Some of the reporters drove into the base in a truck like that one used in the Beirut bombing. They were not stopped. The truck was not searched. They were not asked for identification. Others on the team motored up to the waterfront base in a small boat, docked, and knocked on the door of one of the residences. A member of the team was allowed in to use the bathroom when the door was opened. The journalists took pictures of themselves in various locations and planted notes in others to provide evidence of where they had "infiltrated" the base. Before they went out on their investigative assignment, they had constructed two different ledes for the news story they would write after their investigation. One lede assumed successful infiltration; the other assumed that security was good and they were caught in their failed infiltration. They were successful. The journalists called military leaders for their comments before publishing the results of their investigation.

The example passes the harm-to-harm analysis. The harm caused by the deception was minimal. No innocent person was deceived. Presumably, every person who worked on that military base, whether they were civilian or military, was tasked with keeping the base secure from intruders—pseudo-terrorists or not. The harm caused if the deception had not taken place is far more substantial. Obviously, the base would have been open to infiltration from real terrorists, capable of carrying out pain, death, and destruction.

The second required test for acts that pass the test of consent, convention, paternalism, or harm-to-harm is that of publicity. As morality is a public system—a set of basic rules of engagement that we expect everyone to follow—it is important that exceptions to the rule be publicly known. The *Wilmington Star* illustrates this well. The news organization was prepared to publish a story about its attempted infiltration of the military base, whether or not the journalists were successful. Deceptive acts based on paternalism should be publicly disclosed once the initial event has passed. In the case provided above, news organizations that withheld governmental concerns about the damn about to fail and the ability to get everyone out in time prevented panic. The intensity of the situation could be told after the fact, with an explanation of why that information was initially withheld.

Disclosure, Surveillance, and Physical-World Identity

Imagine that you spent part of yesterday studying your class notes at a desk in your campus library. You yawned. You stretched. You smiled. You scratched your nose while you drew a line through important text with a yellow highlighter. All the while, you were under surveillance. Someone noted when you took a bathroom break and when you walked to the coffee shop, what you ordered, and when you returned to your work. When you closed your window shades at the end of the day, your watcher stopped listing and timing your activities. That list of all of the day's observable behaviors was then slipped into a file that added to your profile.

Most people would demand to know why such information was being recorded about them. What is the purpose? What is the intended use? What all is in that file? If you were able to confront the one who watched you that day, or any of the hundreds of watchers who followed you throughout the years of your life, you would find that there was no particular plan in gathering years of data about you and no specific use. It might be useful to someone someday for some reason. Bits of information or your entire profile had been sold from time to time without your knowledge. And no, it would not be possible for you to get a copy of the file for your own purposes, nor can you defend or explain anything recorded there. You are not allowed to correct mistakes. Nor will you ever profit from the disclosures about you.

This scenario is likely to make most people feel very uncomfortable. It is intrusion. In most countries, it is a violation of privacy for someone to stalk a private individual like this in the physical world.

Yet, all users of digital technology have given permission to be watched like this. And, the watching is more pervasive in the virtual world than it would be in the physical world. In addition to all observable actions, digital data collectors also know with whom users text or correspond with on e-mail. They know users' followers and friends on social media. In fact, when users sign up for a new app, an initial request is often to access the user's contacts.

News organizations in the pre-Internet era didn't know if the newspaper delivered to one's doorstep was read or not or if the television tuned to the local news show was being watched or not. Now legacy media know how long users spend looking at a particular news story on their mobile device and whether they scroll down through the story or glance at the headline and click on.

The difference between the physical and virtual worlds is not just that it is far easier to collect virtual data, compared to the difficulty and expense of hiring physical-world watchers. The major difference is consent. Users of digital technology generally have consented to disclose far more information about themselves than they are aware. As the consents are incremental, no one is aware of the full tally of information that they have agreed to provide over time.

Nevertheless, information is compiled, sold, and used to build a consumer profile more complete than hours of psychological testing could provide.

While news organizations' advertising revenue has plummeted in the move from analog to digital platforms, the reason for that loss in revenue is not an inability for news sites to provide demographic information to advertisers so that they can best target consumers. News sites mine as much data as they can on their users. Their problem is that so many other sites, upon which users are more active than legacy news sites, are targeting users better.

Drones, Social Media Sourcing, Cyber-Lurking

In the physical world, in the United States, and many other democratic nations, journalists are generally not ethically required to identify themselves in public spaces. They can collect and use whatever they see or hear or record in public space and what they find in public documents, without the permission of the story sub-ject or source. Is "public space" in the virtual world a difference of degree from that in the physical world, or is it a difference in kind? The answer to that question is ethically relevant for determining reasonable expectations for how journalists should gather information in the virtual world.

Over the centuries, notions of privacy have constricted in reaction to advancing technology. Taking people's pictures in public spaces without permission is not a legal invasion of privacy. What the Google Maps camera catches as it drives by, collecting images for Google Street View, is also not a violation. But spaces behind tall fences, shuttered windows, and closed doors are still in the realm of physically private spaces. Public space has been traditionally considered to be space where an individual voluntarily ventures out, with the knowledge that what he or she shares there—physical form and any utterance, transaction, or expression—is accessible by unknown members of a mass audience. One may not expect to be captured by Google Maps while retrieving the morning paper from the front steps, but a person who ventured out the front door knows that he or she is visible to others. Going out into public in the physical world provides consent to be viewed.

Drones (http://diydrones.com/) have pushed the privacy envelope in the physical world. These small, mechanical, flying video recorders can go where no uninvited human body can tread. They hop privacy fences, linger over backyard pools and hot tubs, and peer into windows not visible from the street. They create sequences of photos that extend over time. It is not clear how any nation's regulation will ultimately answer when drones used commercially or "recreationally" will need to be justified. As journalists in many countries legally and ethically operate without any special license, a blogger who collects no salary from writing his blog may be classified as a recreational drone user, even if his images run very publicly and persistently in the virtual world.

Yet there are undoubtedly ways in which drones could provide the best and most up-to-date news coverage. Karen McIntyre, who presented at the 2012 Online News Association conference, said drones could be better newsgathering tools than helicopters because drones are significantly cheaper and quieter, don't require extensive pilot training, and can be flown under five hundred feet. Drones "also allow journalists access to places that are dangerous or unreachable, and they provide an aerial view that captures images in ways that photographs taken from the ground cannot" (McIntyre 2015, 160). At the time of this writing, law and ethical conventions regarding journalistic drones are still in development.

However, the Professional Society of Drone Journalists has published a code of ethics. (http://www.dronejournalism.org/code-of-ethics/)

In the virtual world, information about individuals can be quickly found with no involvement of a human story source or subject. But information on the Internet may not be true. Social media profiles are suspect because the sources of information are suspect. A Facebook post describing an individual is likely to carry the heavily-biased agenda of the person posting. A false representation repeated hundreds of times is still a lie. Even a person's online self-description is a snapshot of that person's perspective at that point in time; it is not reflective of how that person might describe him- or herself in any other context. The DOIT analysis process cautions that the information offered is only as good as the sources behind it. It is ethically required for journalists to develop the truest information possible. That means that it is ethically required to report beyond what can be found online and disclose to readers the sources of information.

Journalists also engage with sources online, collecting perspectives from people engaged in discussions about controversial matters. If the discussion is public, such as those attached to news stories on aggregator sites, Twitter or other social media, or news sites, one can assume that the individuals intend for what they say to be shared with a mass audience. There is no ethical problem with journalists gathering information on a public platform. It is not unusual for a tweet posted by an eyewitness at an unfolding event to draw attention from multiple news sites, asking for the user to Direct Message (DM) them for further exclusive contact. If the journalist can verify the source's credibility, at-the-scene sourcing may be developed without the source ever having to disclose his or her physical-world identity.

Journalistic Disclosure and the Eternal Internet

In the days when all news stories were printed products, physically stored and retrieved, clip files languished in file cabinets and videotapes sat on shelves gathering dust, in what news organizations called "the morgue." Once published, clipped, and filed, stories rarely were looked at again unless those named in the story surfaced in some later newsworthy event. And then they resurfaced only if the reporter thought to check the clip file. The initial story, available to news organization staff, was not seen in public after the initial publication. Now stories published long ago, even those published long before the digital era, are available to anyone who fills in the right keywords in a search engine request.

This is an ethical issue because "the permanent memory bank of the Web increasingly means there are no second chances—no opportunities to escape a scarlet letter in your digital past. Now the worst thing you've done is often the first thing everyone knows about you" (Rosen 2010).

In North America and Australia, the freedom to publish overrides what the European Union calls the individual's "right to be forgotten." The Right to be Forgotten, decided by the European Union's Court of Justice in 2014, found that "Individuals have the right—under certain conditions—to ask search engines to remove links with personal information about them. This applies where information is inaccurate, inadequate, irrelevant or excessive for the purposes of data processing.... At the same time, the Court explicitly clarified that the right to be forgotten is not absolute but will always need to be balanced against other fundamental rights, such as the freedom of expression and of the media. A case-by-case assessment is needed considering the type of information in question, its sensitivity for the individual's private life and the interest of the public in having access to that information" (European Commission 2014). In the EU, individuals have the right to ask that search engine companies and owners of web sites where information originated to remove information about them. They can successfully seek that a story be "unpublished" with the law on their side. In the United States, news organizations decide for themselves whether to ever unpublish a story. Most of the requests for stories to be removed are from individuals who believe that the identification causes personal harm that outweighs the importance of the story in the long-term public record. Most media organizations in the United States have decided against unpublishing true information, regardless of harm.

A survey of 110 editors from members of the Associated Press Managing Editors found that very few editors believed that a news organization should unpublish stories. Fewer than 20% of them thought that a story should be withdrawn because, "The article contains outdated information that while accurate could be damaging to the source's reputation in the community," and only 10.4% of those surveyed agreed that a news organization should unpublish a story over "concerns that the post contains private information" (English 2009).

The easiest time to make determinations about whether material should be published is, of course, prior to initial publication. For example, in October 2013, managers at national and local news organizations separately decided whether to publish the names of two girls, twelve and fourteen years old at the time, "who were charged with a felony in online bullying related to a suicide." While it was legal for the sheriff's office to release the names, news organizations had the choice of whether to identify these children. In this case, the *New York Times* and *Associated Press* chose not to publish the children's names. Other news organizations did publish the names.

Publication that identifies children haunt them into their adulthood. In March 2014, the *Tampa Bay Times* chose to publish the name of a teenager when it was discovered that his father, a local school board member, had "exploited his public office to inflate his teenage son's academic record in a scam involving take-at-home tests, altered grades and a bogus course description" (Tampa Bay Times 2014). There was no indication in the news story or in the *Times* editorial on the matter that the teenager had any knowledge of his father's wrongdoing. More than a year after the initial publication, a Google search of the teenager's name and location brought stories regarding the father's actions on his son's behalf to the top of the queue. Regardless of his own culpability, the young man was branded with his father's actions into his adulthood, when, presumably, potential employers would see the stories.

News organizations may be inconsistent in deciding whether to publish the names of child victims. In November 2015, the *San Francisco Chronicle* published an *Associated Press* article that named an eighteen-year-old who had been kidnapped by his father when he was a small child and transported out of state; his identity had been hidden from everyone, including himself (Associated Press 2015). Although this boy was not a minor when found, he was when kidnapped. A day earlier, the same news organization published a wire story by the *Washington Post* that didn't name a five-year-old child whose grandfather had intentionally left the child alone with a loaded gun (Washington Post 2015).

News organizations always choose among facts to include in stories. The argument that users may find information elsewhere does not justify any news organization's particular choice to publish. Each news site has the ethical responsibility to make choices of what to publish, and whether to ever unpublish, based on the importance of the information to the community as a whole as weighed against the consequence to the community if that particular piece of information is not made available.

Applying the DOIT Process to Deception

Let's apply DOIT analysis to journalistic deception as discussed in this chapter:

1. Does the information communicated meet the epistemic normative standards of truth or at least truthfulness?

    If the consideration is deception in the gathering of information, it must pass the tests described above. Can the deception be justified by consent, convention, paternalism, or harm-to-harm analysis? If so, can it also pass the publicity test? If the consideration is deception in presentation, it is never ethically permitted for journalists to engage in active deception——that is, to publish information that intentionally misleads readers to a false conclusion.

    Whether withholding information counts as deception can be determined by asking the following:

    A. Does withholding the information withheld violate a role-related responsibility? For example, citizens don't need to

know, for self-governance, the name of a minor victimized
or, in most cases, participated in criminal acts.

B. Does the information withheld break a promise? Promises
should almost always be kept.

C. Is it illegal for the journalist to withhold the information
from users? (As journalists do not have a legal requirement
to publish anything, the answer to this question is "No".)

D. Does withholding the information constitute cheating? That
is, do users have a reasonable expectation that a journalist
would tell them the withheld information?

If the answers to A through D are "No," then no deception
has occurred. If the answer to one or more of them is "Yes,"
then the publicity test——the willingness of those acting
deceptively to share that publicly——is also required for the
act to be justified.

2. Does the information provided meet the standards of independence
and objectivity?

The publicity test guarantees that the answer to this question will
be obvious in the disclosure.

3. Is the *source* of the information verifiable on the basis of reliable,
trustworthy, and independent corroborative evidence?

This is where special care needs to be taken in gathering online
information. Further digging needs to be done before a journalist
can understand the truthfulness of the information found online.

4. Is the evidence itself provided by the source of the disseminated
information reliable and trustworthy?

Evidence may be impossible to find if a journalist has only pseudonymous online sources.

5. In the case where the truth of the information communicated
cannot be ascertained with certainty, determine whether its truthfulness can at least be established with a reasonable probability

based on the disseminator's credibility, reliability, independence, and trustworthiness.

It is likely that this hurdle is rarely cleared by reliance on previously published online material. As harm to story subjects happens in the physical world, the basis upon which a journalist publishes potentially harmful information must also usually rely on the disseminator's physical-world credibility. The exception is in real-time news coverage of an unfolding event with an eyewitness who is communicating through Twitter or equivalent social media. Journalists must verify the source's location and ability to provide credible on-the-scene material, but in these rare cases, physical-world identity of the source may not be relevant.

6. Finally, determine if the information disseminated supports or violates the rights to freedom and well-being of any agents, including story subjects, sources, or users.

Withholding the names of children or vulnerable others may support the freedom and well-being of those story subjects without violating the freedom or well-being of users. Unpublishing similar information, long after the fact, with an appended editor's note that an individual's identity was withdrawn on the same freedom and well-being justification is ethically permitted or may be ethically required.

Early in the chapter, we noted that some believe that the Internet has turned us all into liars. The "terms and conditions" to which one must click "I have read and agree," are posted to protect the web site owner's liability. If an individual violates a policy or objects to stated use of data, the Web manager has a signed document to show user agreement. The interesting philosophical question is whether the user who clicks, "I have read and agree," without having read the terms and conditions is, in fact, acting with the intent to mislead anyone. Some studies have found that as few as 7% of users have ever read the document to which they agreed. Some activists urge users to join them in confessing and protesting what they call the biggest lie on the web (http://www.biggestlie.com/).

Questions for Reflection

1   *Think through times when you have chosen not to tell particular people certain information. Did you act deceptively? If so, was the deception justified?*

2   *Think about times that you have actively deceived—intentionally led others to a false conclusion. With the wisdom of hindsight, come up with alternatives you might have used rather than deceive.*

3   *Take a look at the pieces of information that are available about you on the Internet. How would a profile written about you based on your online persona be different from that based on who you know yourself to be in the physical world?*

4   *Identify spaces in the physical world that are clearly public and that are clearly private. Identify areas in between. Now, do the same for the virtual world. Do you have any private space on the Internet? If so, how is that constituted and protected?*

Works Cited

"Alberta Code of Ethics." *Accountable Journalism.* Accessed November 17, 2015. https://accountablejournalism.org/ethics-codes/Canada-Alberta.

Associated Press. 2015. "Alabama Child Missing Since 2002 Found in Ohio." *San Francisco Chronicle*, November 6.

"Australia/Oceania: APN News & Media: Editorial Code Of Ethics." *Accountable Journalism.* Accessed November 16, 2015. https://accountablejournalism.org/ethics-codes/editorial-code-of-ethics.

"Australian Press Council Privacy Code." *Accountable Journalism.* Accessed November 17, 2015. https://accountablejournalism.org/ethics-codes/Australia-APC-Privacy.

"Canadian Assocation of Journalists' Statement of Principles." *Accountable Journalism.* Accessed November 16, 2015. https://accountablejournalism.org/ethics-codes/Canada-CAJ-Principles.

Elliott, D. 1991. "On Deceiving One's Source." *The International Journal of Applied Philosophy* 6 (1).

Elliott, D. and C. Culver 1992. "Defining and Analyzing Journalistic Deception." *Journal of Mass Media Ethics* 7 (2).

English, K. 2009. "The Long Tail of News: To Unpublish or Not to Unpublish." APME.

European Commission. 2014. "Factsheet on the 'Right to be Forgotten' Ruling." *European Commission*. Accessed October 23, 2015. http://ec.europa.eu/justice/data-protection/files/factsheets/factsheet_data_protection_en.pdf.

McIntyre, K. 2015. "How Current Law Might Apply to Drone Journalism." *Newspaper Research Journal* 36 (2): 158–169.

Rosen, J. 2010. "The Web Means the End of Forgetting." *New York Times*, July 21. Accessed July 25, 2010. http://www.nytimes.com/2010/07/25/magazine/25privacy-tw.html.

Tampa Bay Times. 2014. "Get to Bottom of Rigged Grades." *Tampa Bay Times*, March 5: 8A.

The Washington Post. 2015. "Grandfather Leaves Child With Loaded Gun, Sheriff Says." November 3.

9

Media Corruption

In this chapter, we shall examine and explore the presence of **corruption** in the media by reference to Plato's myth of Gyges (https://en.wikipedia.org/wiki/ring_of_gyges), as this has contemporary significance and relevance in explaining corruption in the media at present. The main dialogue of Plato that will be referred to is the *Republic* (http://classics.mit.edu/Plato/republic.html) (Plato 1952).

The primary objective of this chapter is to identify and categorize the different types of media corruption, the ways in which these are caused, and the contexts in which they manifest in current physical and virtual media environments and practices. Whereas much has been written on other forms of corruption, including corporate, political, and police corruption, media corruption has been largely, overlooked. Although identified as unethical within the general corpus of media ethics, practices such as *cash-for-comment* and media release journalism, including *video news releases* (VNRs), *fake news, staged news, advertorials,* and *infomercials,* among others, have not been commonly defined as corrupt practices. In addition, there has been no systematic theoretical study of why and how such practices constitute corruption. The reason for this oversight is partly that the concept of corruption itself is not well understood or clearly defined; even when corruption is defined, it is often narrowly defined, for example in terms of corporate financial misfeasance as in the case of Enron (https://en.wikipedia.org/wiki/enron_scandal), or abuse of

Ethics for a Digital Era, First Edition. Deni Elliott and Edward H. Spence.
© 2018 John Wiley & Sons Ltd. Published 2018 by John Wiley & Sons Ltd.

political and public office for private gain, as in the case of Watergate (https://en.wikipedia.org/wiki/watergate_scandal).

Starting with a conceptual and philosophical analysis of corruption in general, first developed by Edward Spence with Seumas Miller and Peter Roberts (2005) and then developed further and applied specifically to the phenomenon of media corruption by Edward Spence (Spence 2008), a co-author of this book, the chapter will provide an applied philosophical model of corruption that will be utilized to identify and categorize major types of corruption that arise in the media. Some key case studies will provide a practical illustration and contextualization of those major types of media corruption.

After outlining a few of the main types of corruption in the media, the chapter will focus on an analysis and ethical evaluation of just one of these types of corruption: Cash-for-Comment. It will be argued that this practice, which passes on paid-for comment or information as journalistic comment or news, constitutes deception and is thus ethically objectionable. Moreover, this chapter argues that this practice also constitutes corruption. Specifically, it is an example of corruption of the public communication and information processes, the integrity of which are vital to the democratic system and the rights of citizens to be informed about matters of public interest truthfully and fairly.

A Tale of Corruption: The Myth of Gyges

Once upon a time, a certain shepherd from Lydia named Gyges, while tending to his sheep, found a ring. He soon discovered that by turning the ring on his finger, he could make himself invisible. A few days later, he went to the palace with a delegation of shepherds to see the king. By making himself invisible, he seduced the queen, killed the king, and assumed total power by becoming the king himself. Another character, Glaucon, continues the story by asking us to imagine an ordinary putative person who, like Gyges, has the ability through possession of a similar magical ring to render him- or herself invisible. Invisibility would allow that person the opportunity to act unethically at will with total impunity.

Glaucon refers to this possibility as the "highest reach of injustice, being deemed just when you are not." He labels this "the most perfect injustice" (Plato 1952). Given such a possibility, what possible reason would someone like Gyges have for not being corrupt but being non-corrupt and moral instead? The question of "why be moral" under Gygean conditions of perfect injustice is referred to in the ethics literature as the "authoritative question of morality-" (Gewirth 1978). The philosophical debate as to whether a compelling answer can be given to that question is still ongoing. We address that question in the concluding chapter of this book.

The Characterizing Features of Corruption

Five features that emerge from an examination of the myth of Gyges in Plato's *Republic*, that seem, at least initially, to characterize corruption, are: the possession of power, a disposition to exercise that power, an opportunity to exercise that power, invisibility or concealment, and self-regarding gain.

We will define *possession of power* as the ability or capacity to act in a manner capable of bringing about a certain intended desired outcome; a *disposition to exercise that power* as the possession of a predisposition, pro-attitude, or willingness to purposefully exercise that power; *opportunity* as having the opportunity, either presented to oneself or engineered by oneself, to engage in some activity for which one has the power and the predisposition in which to engage; and *invisibility* or *concealment* as the ability or quality an agent has for keeping the motives and the identity of the agency of his actions invisible, concealed, or hidden from the gaze of others. *Self-regarding gain* is any gain, not necessarily financial, that accrues to the agent personally or to a group of which he is a member, as a result of his or the group's actions. With regard to the condition of invisibility, while the actions themselves would be visible at least with regard to their effects and consequences, the identity of their agency is invisible. Or at least the corrupt agent's intention is to keep his agency invisible or concealed.

Many of the characterizing features of corruption are present and accompany nearly all acts of corruption. For without power, one cannot commit a corrupt act. Possessing power is not enough; one must have the disposition to exercise that power willingly. Similarly, through lack of opportunity, one cannot engage in corrupt activity, even when one has both the power and the disposition to act corruptly. Invisibility seems to also be a characterizing feature of corruption that is usually, if not always, present in instances of corrupt activity.

Invisibility seems to be at least instrumentally desirable, for without invisibility, one might not be able to evade detection, which is essential to escape possible social disapproval and punitive retribution from others or the state. Even for a Gyges-likeperson, keeping the identity of his agency in committing the immoral acts hidden would be prudent, lest he invoke social disapproval, which may eventually undermine his power to rule and invite retribution from those he harms through his unethical conduct. Like Glaucon's perfectly unjust person, perfectly corrupt persons maintain an outward appearance of probity, justice, and morality, while carrying out their corrupt deeds in secret. In this way they maximize their self-regarding gain, which can accrue to them personally or to a group to which they belong or cause to which they are committed, with little or no instrumental cost to themselves, their group, or their cause.

Sometimes the corruption of deeds and character may remain invisible even to the corrupt agents themselves. The invisibility may be self-induced through self-justifying rationalizations; ignorance may be manifested and expressed as lack of self-reflection and self-knowledge. Usually, self-justifying rationalizations and ignorance are closely related. For often it is ignorance—a lack of self-examination and self-reflection—that necessitates self-justifying rationalizations on the part of the corrupt agent.

Though the five features described normally accompany typical cases of corruption, they are nevertheless not sufficient to fully characterize corruption. If they were, a house burglar or a professional bank robber would be deemed corrupt. However, though immoral, the actions of the house burglar and bank robber are not what we would normally describe as corrupt. The missing condition is a socially pre-established and widely acknowledged fiduciary relationship of trust that exists between the corrupt person or corrupt group and the person or group of persons who are harmed in some way by the corrupt person's or the corrupt group's actions.

This prior fiduciary relationship of trust does not normally exist between the burglar and the bank robber and those who are harmed by their actions, namely, the homeowners or the banks and their customers. So, violation of fiduciary duty is the sixth characterizing feature of corruption.

The fiduciary relationship can be articulated in political, professional, social, or familial terms; and the self-regarding gain is not always financial or material. Thus a priest, minister of religion, or teacher who sexually abuses children in his or her care is acting corruptly, even though there might not be any financial gain.

The following sections present key illustrative examples of major types of media communication messages which, insofar as they possess the six characterizing features of corruption discussed above and are designed to mislead and in some cases deceive their targeted audiences, constitute corruption. These illustrative cases although somewhat dated now have been chosen because of their timeless significance and importance in highlighting how such cases constitute *typical cases* of media corruption.

Types of Media Corruption

The Enemy Within: Fictional News, Biased News, and News for Sale

Fictional news: two central cases, those of Jayson Blair (https:// en.wikipedia.org/wiki/jayson_blair) of the *New York Times* and Stephen Glass (https://en.wikipedia.org/wiki/stephen_glass) of the *New Republic,* are illustrative examples of this type of internal corruption.

Both wrote fabricated stories, mixing fact with fiction, and presented them as news. For example, among the fabricated stories written by then-*New York Times* reporter Jayson Blair was an interview with the parents of Jessica Lynch, the Iraqi prisoner of war freed by US troops. The story later proved to be entirely a product of Blair's fertile imagination. Ironically, the veracity of the reporting of the rescue of Private Jessica Lynch itself came under doubt and media scrutiny with regard to whether the incident happened as reported or whether it was staged by the US military spin machine as political propaganda.

Biased news: Robert Greenwald's documentary *Outfoxed: Rupert Murdoch's War on Journalism* (https://en.wikipedia.org/wiki/outfoxed) raises searching questions about corporate influence in the media and in particular the right-wing political agenda of News Corporation's *Fox News,* and, as such, provides an illustrative case study for bias in the media and its conduciveness to corruption. Another illustrative case study involves CBS anchor Dan Rather, who has admitted that the authenticity of the documents he used to question President Bush's National Guard record in his *60 Minutes* program was questionable. Was this a case of a genuine mistake, sloppy journalism, or a deliberate attempt to skew the news? This case might provide an illuminating analysis of how bias, even when not intentionally used to slant the news, might lead to biased news though negligence. Insofar as negligence in reporting meets the characterizing features of corruption, it can be argued that it is a form of corruption. Negligence meets the characterizing features of corruption because is a dereliction of duty. The journalist's duty is to inform the public on matters of public interest truthfully and reliably.

Yet another form of media corruption by biased reporting is that involving the use of *unidentified sources.* Given the media's ability and willingness to use and sometimes exploit unnamed sources, are there cases where such undisclosed sources, although authentic, are deliberately used to generate biased reporting with a political agenda? The Judith Miller-Valerie Plame (https://en.wikipedia.org/wiki/judith_miller) case study shows that this is an illustrative case of unnamed sources being used for biased political reasons.

In addition, are there cases where the undisclosed sources are the product of "creative journalism," made up to tell a particular story that serves the media organization's political or social agenda? One case concerning the creation and use of an "unidentified source" to tell a biased story, one that turned out to be entirely false, involved the *Daily Express.* The gist of the story was that "a suspected Al Qaeda plot to target Tony Blair's home has been foiled…" (*Daily Express,* August 16, 2004). The source of the story was unidentified "security sources." However, just hours after the story was published, the Durham police categorically denied the authenticity of the story. According to them, the whole incident involved a couple of Lithuanians in a stolen Vauxhall, who had been picked up by police a few miles from Blair's house, not at the time reported in the *Daily Express* article but a year earlier. Not dissuaded by the British police's denial concerning the authenticity of the story, News Corp newspapers throughout Australia published similar stories: "Plot to kill Blair foiled—Al Qaeda linked to assassination plan" (*Daily Telegraph*, August 17, 2004), and others like it.

News for sale: Advertorials or infomercials exemplify another type of corruption that is generated from within journalism itself. It usually involves the selling of pseudo "editorials" or "news" as part of an overall advertising package by media organizations in the forms of both print and broadcast journalism. At least one case study that indicates this type of media corruption involved a Sydney suburban newspaper, the *Sydney Weekly Courier,* that offered professionals, business people, and even candidates in local council elections advertising packages that included the sale of four ads with three complimentary "editorials" written by the clients themselves. In all cases, there was no disclosure by the *Courier* that these texts, presented as editorials, were a form of advertising or advertorials. In its defense when exposed by *Media Watch*, a weekly program of the Australian Broadcasting Corporation (ABC) that monitors and reports on the ethical blunders and lapses of the Australian media, the *Courier* replied that the complimentary advertising pieces were separated from other news and editorial content by their labeling as a "Special Feature."

Although smaller in scale and perhaps significance than other forms of media corruption, this type of corruption is pervasive and typically indicative of the ill effects of the commercialization of media on the proper role of journalism: informing the public as citizens, truthfully and fairly, on matters of public interest. Simply put, advertorials and infomercials are a perversion and a corruption of that important civic role.

A more substantial and well-known example of this type of corruption is the case involving the *Los Angeles Times* and the Staples Center. Back in 1999, the journalists assigned to write a story on the new Staples Center sports arena for a special issue of the Sunday magazine, were unaware that the publisher of the *Times* had agreed to split the advertising revenue from the issue with the Staples Center. The article was published without disclosing the *Times's* financial interest in the reported story.

Sleeping With the Enemy: Fake News, Staged News, and Cash-for-Comment

This type of media corruption is the result of collusion, intentional at worst and negligent at best, between journalists and public relations and advertising organizations or government agencies. This is perhaps one of the most insidious and pervasive forms of media corruption. It not only corrupts the communication of information processes and products, but more nefariously, it corrupts the institutional processes of the democratic system itself. It harms every citizen both individually and collectively, as it violates their fundamental right to make informed choices on the basis of accurate information that is free of deception and manipulation.

Fake news: "Over a ten-month period, the Center for Media and Democracy (CMD) documented television newsrooms' use of 36 video news releases (VNRs)—a small sample of the thousands produced each year. CMD identified 77 television stations, from those in the largest to the smallest markets, that aired these VNRs or related satellite media tours (SMTs) in 98 separate instances, without disclosure to viewers [that the information was produced by those with private interests rather than by journalists]. Collectively, these 77 stations reach more than half of the U.S. population. The VNRs and SMTs whose broadcast CMD documented were produced by three broadcast PR firms for 49 different clients, including General Motors, Intel, Pfizer and Capital One. In each case, these 77 television stations actively disguised the sponsored content to make it appear to be their own reporting. In almost all cases, stations failed to balance the clients' messages with independently-gathered footage or basic journalistic research. More than one-third of the time, stations aired the pre-packaged VNR in its entirety."

The above passage, published on the web site of the *Center for Media and Democracy* (http://www.prwatch.org/) and written by Diane Farsetta and Daniel Price (Center for Media and Democracy 2006), highlights an ever-increasing trend of using media releases, including video news releases (VNRs), by public relations organizations to promote and publicize their clients' products, services, or interests in the form of pseudo-"objective and independent news stories" without no or insufficient disclosure that these are media releases. Designed to look like editorial and journalistic comment in print or broadcast media forms, these hybrids of information and persuasion, what we call *media release journalism* (Simmons and Spence 2006), are designed to deceive by stealth. Starting in college, students in public relations studies are taught how to design sample media releases for clients that look, smell, and feel like the real thing: editorial journalistic columns or segments of broadcast news.

In design as well as execution, the practice of media release journalism has the hallmark of corruption, as illustrated by the myth of Gyges in Plato's *Republic*: they appear just, in that they are misleadingly offered as journalistic accounts; yet they are not—they are designed to advance client interests. The case study involving the US military paying newspapers in Iraq to publish media releases designed to look like journalistic comment and editorial opinion without disclosure that these were paid-for media releases designed merely for propaganda purposes, is one such instance. Another case involved US government departments using PR spokespeople as bogus journalists to promote the government's policies from aviation security to farming. The Bush government also paid real columnists to write in support of administration policies without any disclosure that the columnists had accepted cash-for-comment.

Yet another example of media release journalism is the case involving a campaign to deceive the Australian public orchestrated by an Australian PR consultancy firm on behalf of a client, *Abbott Australasia*, a pharmaceutical company. The unidentified PR firm, for ease of reference let's refer to it as XYZ, targeted several regional newspapers around Australia with the strategic intention that these newspapers, given their known limited staff resources, would in all probability publish its media releases as journalistic opinion pieces. They did. This is a well-known and pervasive PR strategy that targets and uses journalists as "credible third-party endorsers" of their client's paid-for information. (Johnson and Zawawi 2004, 263). Of course the public that receives such information remains, through the absence of a qualifying statement that these are media releases, unaware that the information presented to them as journalistic comment or opinion is, quite often, a word-for-word media release, in some cases with the journalist's byline attached to it for extra credibility.

Staged news: One of the most infamous examples of this type of media corruption is a case that involved the international public relations firm Hill and Knowlton. Just before the first Gulf War of 1991, it staged a fabricated story using the daughter of Kuwait's ambassador in the United States. She posed as a nurse who claimed that she had witnessed Iraqi soldiers in a Kuwait hospital throwing babies out of their incubators, onto the floor, and leaving them to die. That story went a long way in swaying American public opinion and won Congress approval for waging war against Iraq in the first Gulf War (Stauber and Rampton 1995, Chapter 10). A related case was the staging of the fall of Saddam Hussein's statue after the capture of the Iraqi capital by US troops. According to a Marine colonel, the toppling of the statue was not the spontaneous and joyous action of Iraqi civilians, as indicated by the striking TV images that were beamed around the world. Contrary to those images, it was rather a carefully staged event by the US Army's psychological operations team that selected the statue as a "target of opportunity," one that resulted in a brilliant piece of modern-day war propaganda (*Los Angeles Times*, July 3, 2004).

Cash-for-comment: Journalism manifests corruption by sometimes operating under conditions of more or less perfect injustice, both at the level of individual journalists and the level of news corporations and in both print and broadcast journalism. At the individual as well as the corporate levels, journalism will, at times, publicly advocate and endorse its role of serving the public interest by informing the public truthfully and accurately, with balance and fairness—while at the same time undermine the public interest by presenting information to the public that is knowingly untrue, either because it is inaccurate or incomplete and it is biased, unfair, and motivated primarily by money and self-interest rather than morality. Similar to media releases, *cash-for-comment* is a type of media corruption that involves presenting paid advertisements as editorial comment or opinion. Not unlike advertorials which they resemble in presenting paid-for information as editorial comment or news, cash-for-comment cases exemplify the double standards of corrupt journalism that engages in such practices. Armstrong Williams, a prominent black commentator, was paid $240,000 by the Bush administration to promote the government's "No Child Left Behind" (NCLB) education law reform policy, in the hope of winning support among black families. The deal required Williams to "regularly comment on NCLB during the course of his broadcasts" and to interview Education Secretary Rod Paige for TV and radio spots that aired during the show in 2004 (Toppo, 2005). The deal with Williams was only part of a $1 million package with the public relations firm Ketchum that included the use of VNRs to promote the government's NCLB nationwide. The Bush administration had also used VNRs designed to look like news reports to promote its Medicare prescription drug plan the previous year.

In Britain, Professor Roger Scruton, a famous and influential philosopher known for his provocative and controversial opinions on smoking and fox hunting, among other things, was exposed for receiving money without disclosure in support of the tobacco industry in weekly columns in the *Wall Street Journal* and the *Financial Times*. Following exposure, he was dismissed from both publications. This was a far cry from Plato's *philosopher kings* who according to Plato should always act independently of personal gain or interest in safeguarding and promoting the citizens' rights to freedom, well-being and the truth!

Corruption in the New Digital Media

How might corruption manifest itself in the new digital media? Are the sources, content, and the technologies of the new digital media themselves less or more liable to corruption than those in the old corporate media? It could turn out that the situation is more complex still, namely, that the new media are less liable to certain forms of corruption and more liable to other forms of corruption. For example, web blogs can be used covertly by advertisers and public relations practitioners to generate cash-for-comment, media release journalism, and advertorials, as well as *product placements*, by misrepresenting paid-for information or advertising as independent editorial comment or opinion. Insofar as advertorials, infomercials, media release journalism, and cash-for-comment practices are types of media corruption, then similar practices that occur in the new digital media also constitute corruption and are thus ethically objectionable.

At least one example concerning a cash-for-comment case involved the digital media was that of Marqui, a company in Vancouver, that paid bloggers, who claimed to be independent, to mention the company. A prediction in the UK *Guardian Unlimited* that the Internet would overtake national newspapers in the competition for advertising spending proved correct (Buckland, 2006; Poynter.org (http://www.poynter.org/news/75514/uk-net-advertising-to-overtake-newspapers-by-end-of-2006/)), which means that the use of blogs and other digital media will increasingly become an attractive and lucrative target for advertising spam and public relations spin. We can expect more and different types of media corruption in the ever expanding cyberspace.

Another case of a blogger misleading her audience is that of the Australian blogger Belle Gibson (http://www.theguardian.com/australia-news/2015/apr/22/none-of-its-true-wellness-blogger-belle-gibson-admits-she-never-had-cancer). Gibson started a digital community and sold recipe books based on her claims that she cured herself of terminal brain cancer through diet and lifestyle. Upon further media investigation she was, however, obliged to admit that she lied about having cancer and her claims that her diet cured her of cancer were in fact, untrue. We can think of this case as another example of a cash-for-comment case, as Gibson sold her diet book to her online community on false claims and misinformation.

It is worth mentioning here that given our understating of *media convergence*, which we explored in Chapter 6, the dissemination of information on the Internet, which involves no sharp distinction in principle between information communicated by legacy journalists and by everyone else who communicates *information* to an intended audience, such as citizen-journalists, bloggers, and so on, the Belle Gibson's cash-for-comment case highlights the important point of how media corruption can arise also and prominently in media convergent communication practices. The Dual Obligation Information Theory (DOIT) that we examined in Chapter 5, demonstrates that everyone who communicates information to an intended audience is committed to the same ethical and epistemic principles and standards as legacy journalists.

Cash-for- Posts (http://www.smh.com.au/technology/web-culture/cash-for-posts-the-murky-ethics-of-social-media-stardom-20151105-gkrs29.html) and Cash-for-Tweets (http://www.crikey.com.au/2012/04/24/tweet-for-your-supper-the-new-wave-of-cash-for-comment/), where celebrity social media personalities get paid-for endorsement of products and services on social media sites such as Instagram and Twitter without disclosure to their thousands of followers that their endorsements are paid for by marketing and advertising promoters, is becoming common practice. Nondisclosure of paid comment is misleading and a form of deception. Clearly, then, it is ethically objectionable on the basis of DOIT. The information communicated is neither reliable nor trustworthy, since its source, namely, the paid endorser, is not unencumbered and independent but undisclosed paid-for-comment. However, even if unethical, does it constitute media corruption? This is a very interesting question, one we ask our readers to explore further for themselves.

One way of thinking about this issue is that it all depends on whether the social media endorser (who is not a journalist but a social media commentator) has a *fiduciary duty of trust*, as in the case of a journalist, to inform his or her followers and readers with truthful, reliable, and trustworthy information or comment. Given the fluidity between journalists, bloggers, tweeters, and other social media commentators in the convergent digital media of today, perhaps one could make a case that this is a form of information corruption. However, it could be argued that it is not of the same degree as serious media corruption that impacts on matters of public interest, such as information concerning government, education, health, and matters of state.

A Detailed Analysis of a Case Study of Media Corruption

Cash-for-Comment: A Case of Corruption

In what has come to be known in Australia as the "The Cash-for-Comment case," John Laws, a well-known Australian radio celebrity, abused his editorial power in 2001 for the purpose of influencing the opinion of his 2 million listeners toward a group of banks for a sum of $1.2 million. The financial transaction between Laws and the banks was carried out in secret and concealed from the public, including his audience. Just a few weeks prior to his deal with the banks, Laws had repeatedly criticized the banks on his radio program for acting unethically in imposing unjustified bank fees on their customers and cutting back on vital services.

Laws' favorable comments on the banking sector, following the $1.2 million deal, can be seen as an instance of an advertorial. The public, including Laws' listeners, was led to think that Laws was expressing a genuinely unbiased and informed view about the banks, when in effect, and unbeknown to the public and his listeners, he was advertising the banks' "merits" for a price, offering editorial comment for cash. In the United States, the "Cash for Editorial Comment" phenomenon is known as "Payola."

John Laws' cash-for-comment case counts as a form of corruption because it displays all six features of corruption described earlier in this chapter. Laws had the power, the disposition, and the opportunity; he kept the deal of the $1.2 million payment from the banks invisible from the public and his listeners; he did it for a self-regarding gain (money); and he violated a fiduciary duty of trust which he owed to his listeners. Moreover, Laws did all this while pretending to be informing the public and his audience about matters that were in their best interest. He had, over the years, developed a reputation as a defender and guardian of the "battlers" against a public scourge of corrupt or merely inept politicians and civil servants. Without too much exaggeration, he packaged himself as the champion of the working-class people. Laws, in other words, like Glaucon's perfectly unjust person, appeared just when he was, if our analysis is right, both unjust and corrupt, at least in this particular instance.

Applying DOIT to further evaluate this case, we can also claim that John Laws' cash-for-comment case violated the epistemic and ethical conditions for the dissemination of information. First, because the information he communicated to his audience about the Australian banks was misinformation, not information, it was misleading, unreliable, and untrustworthy. Second, the paid-for comments he made to his audience about the banks violated their rights to freedom and well-being because the misinformation he provided under the guise of reliable and trustworthy information about the banks undermined the ability of his audience to arrive at a reliable and trustworthy judgment concerning a matter of public interest.

Questions for Reflection

1   What are the essential characterizing features of media corruption?
2   Do the features that characterize media corruption apply equally to both offline and online media?
3   Do all or just some cases of cash-for-comment examples constitute media corruption, and if so, why? What about the Belle Gibson case cited above?
4   Why is media corruption epistemically and ethically objectionable?
5   Can you identify further types of media corruption not identified in this chapter? Describe them and explain why they constitute media corruption.
6   For each of the different types of media corruption described in this chapter can you think of other recent cases that might also fit under those types of media corruption?
7   The article in the attached link *Iran Fake Blog Smear Campaign* (https://www.theguardian.com/world/2013/jan/24/iran-fake-blog-smear-campaign-journalist-bbc) appeared in the UK *Guardian* newspaper. Did the reported practice of creating false and fake information by Iran about Iranian journalists working for the BBC in the United Kingdom constitute media corruption and if so why?
8   A recent case that has attracted wide coverage around the world has become known as *The Panama Papers* (https://en.wikipedia.org/wiki/Panama_Papers) perhaps through allusion to another famous case study of leaked documents that of *The Pentagon Papers* (https://en.wikipedia.org/wiki/Pentagon_Papers). Do you think there is any similarity between these two cases and if so in what sense are they similar? In what sense are they different?
    Do you think that both cases illustrate how good investigative journalism is important in informing citizens on matters of public interest and at least, as in the case of the Panama Papers, crucial in reporting and exposing corruption through the symbiotic and convergent relationship between the 4th Estate and the 5th Estate that we examined in Chapter 6?

Works Cited

Buckland, M. 2006. "UK Net Advertising to 'Overtake Newspapers by End of 2006.'" Poynter.org. Accessed December 21, 2015. http://www.poynter.org/news/75514/uk-net-advertising-to-overtake-newspapers-by-end-of-2006/.

Farsetta, D. and D. Price. 2006. "Fake TV News: Widespread and Undisclosed." Centre for Media and Democracy. http://www.prwatch.org/fakenews/execsummary, 6, April.

Gewirth, A. 1978. *Reason and Morality*. Chicago, IL: University of Chicago Press.

Johnston J. and C. Zawawi (eds.). 2004. "Media Relations." In *Public Relations Theory and Practice* (2nd edition). Allen and Unwin.

Miller, S., P. Roberts, and E. Spence. 2005. *Corruption and Anti-Corruption: An Applied Philosophical Approach*. Upper Saddle River, NJ: Pearson/Prentice Hall.

Plato, 1952. *The Dialogues of Plato*. Translated by Benjamin Jowett. Chicago, IL: Encyclopedia Britannica Inc., Book II: 359–361.

Simmons, P. and E. Spence. 2006. "The Practice and Ethics of Media Release Journalism." *Australian Journalism Review* 28 (1): 167–181.

Spence, E. 2006. *Ethics Within Reason: A Neo-Gewirthian Approach* Lanham, MD: Lexington Books (a division of Rowman and Littlefield).

Spence, E. 2008. "Media Corruption." *International Journal of Applied Philosophy* 22 (2): 231–241.

Stauber, J. and S. Rampton. 1995. *Toxic Sludge Is Good For You: Lies, Damn Lies and the Public Relations Industry*. Monroe, ME: Common Courage Press.

Toppo, G. 2005. "Education Dept. Paid Commentator to Promote law." *USA Today*, July, 1.

Zucchino, D. 2003. "Army Stage-Managed Fall of Hussein Statue." *Los Angeles Times*, July 3.

Part III

Using the Virtual World
to Create a Better Physical World

10

Beyond Ethics

Communicating Wisely

Information, Communication, and Wisdom

In this chapter, we will investigate the differences between information, knowledge, and wisdom, with the aim of examining the significance and relevance of those concepts and their differences for media communication. The chapter begins with a short *philosophy play* (Spence 2008) that highlights dramatically those differences and their importance for the dissemination of media information that not only contributes to knowledge but also to our well-being, both as individuals and as society through communicating wisely.

Wise after the Fact (http://www.greekfestivalofsydney.com.au/festivalI I/events/event_wisdom_info.htm): A One-Act Play

Prologue

From Goethe's *Faust*

> **FAUST:** I've studied now Philosophy
> And Jurisprudence, Medicine
> And even, alas! Theology,—
> From end to end, with labor keen;

And here, poor fool! with all my lore
I stand, no wiser than before:
I'm Magister—yea, Doctor,
And straight or cross-wise, wrong or right,
These ten years long, with many woes,
I've led my scholars by the nose,—
And see, that nothing can be known!
That knowledge cuts me to the bone.
I'm cleverer, true, than those fops of teachers,
Doctors and Magisters, Scribes and Preachers;
Neither scruples nor doubts come now to smite me,
Nor Hell nor Devil can longer affright me.
For this, all pleasure am I foregoing;
I do not pretend to aught worth knowing,
I do not pretend I could be a teacher
To help or convert a fellow-creature.
Then, too, I've neither lands nor gold,
Nor the world's least pomp or honor hold—
No dog would endure such a curst existence!
Wherefore, from Magic I seek assistance,
That many a secret perchance I reach
Through spirit-power and spirit-speech,
And thus the bitter task forego
Of saying the things I do not know,—
That I may detect the inmost force
Which binds the world, and guides its course;
Its germs, productive powers explore,
And rummage in empty words no more!

Ms. Wise (W):	Hi! Are you Mr. Google?
Google (G):	Who's asking?
W:	My name is Wise, Belinda Wise.
G:	Well Ms. Wise, wise you are, you've come to the right place. I am indeed the person you're looking for—Google at your service.
W:	I'm so glad I found you My Google; I have been searching everywhere for you these last few days.

G: Oh, you do surprise me, Ms. Wise—everyone can find me at the touch of a key. I am ubiquitous and ever-present. How can I help you?

W: Oh I do hope you can, Mr. Google, I do hope you can—I am at my wits' end. You see, I have been searching it seems forever and still cannot find that which I'm looking for.

G: Calm yourself, Ms. Wise, please calm yourself; whatever you have been looking for your search is at an end—yes, presently at an end. I will help you find it, and find it you shall—and a lot more besides. There's nothing I do not know, absolutely nothing at all. I know everything there is to know and ever can be known. I know the present and the past, the future and beyond. I know the secrets of the heavens and those of the seven seas; I know of every nook and cranny across the blue-white globe. My knowledge is like the universe: limitless and vast. My spheres of knowledge extend into infinity. I am everywhere, know everything. I am omniscient and omnipresent.

W: Are you sure you're not also God, Mr. Google?

G: Now you mention it, Ms. Wise, I may indeed be God; after all, I do seem to have all his essential qualities. I'm omniscient (I know everything), omnipresent (I am everywhere at once), omnipotent (I am all-powerful), and benevolent to boot (I diligently care for and serve people all over the world).

W: Yeah, right! Keep saying that, and you'll end up burned at the stake for blasphemy, just like that poor fellow Giordano, what's-his-name.

G: Bruno.

W: Yes, exactly.

G: Well, Ms. Wise, I'll take my chances. In the meantime, just ask me anything you wish, and I shall tell you, shall let you know at once. I am Google, at your service.

W: I hope you can, Mr. Google I hope you can. What is wisdom, and where can I find it?

G: Wisdom? Did you say wisdom? That's easy. His full name was Norman Wisdom. He was a British comedian of the 1950s and early 60s.

W: Oh no! I didn't mean that, I didn't mean that at all. I don't see how a British comedian from the 1950s or 60s is going to help me find the meaning to life. No, what I meant is Wisdom, what the Ancient Greeks called Sophia, the art of knowing how to live a good life—you know, like Socrates. By all accounts, he was a wise man. Was he not?

G: Socrates of Athens, philosopher, teacher of Plato, so named because he had a wide back, by all accounts ugly in appearance, married to the shrew Xanthippe— declared by the Oracle of Delphi to be the wisest of mortals; sentenced to death by hemlock on charges of corrupting the young and being irreverent to the gods.

W: Yes, yes, I know all that, but that is simply biographical information about Socrates; it tells me nothing of what wisdom is and how to attain it. Just knowing a lot of facts about Socrates' life is not going to make me wise, is it now?

G: It may save you from disappointment and possibly a painful death. However, if you still want to know about what wisdom is, I can certainly tell you. Why didn't you say so in the first place?

W: Well, I just thought from the way my question was phrased that you would know the difference between British comedy and Socratic wisdom.

G: Ms. Wise, my answers are as good as your questions. Even someone as perfect as I am cannot always compensate for people's imperfections.

Now then wisdom: Wisdom, is defined by Merriam-Webster's Collegiate Dictionary as: 1 a: Accumulated philosophic or scientific learning : knowledge; b: Ability to discern inner qualities and relationships : insight; c: Good sense : judgment 2: A wise attitude, belief, or course of action. 3: The teachings of the ancient wise men.

Most psychologists regard wisdom as distinct from the cognitive abilities measured by standardized *intelligence* (http://en.wikipedia.org/

wiki/intelligence) tests. Wisdom is often considered to be a trait that can be developed by experience but cannot be taught. When applied to practical matters, the term wisdom is synonymous with *prudence* (http://en. wikipedia.org/wiki/prudence). Some see wisdom as a quality that even a child, otherwise immature, may possess, independent of experience or complete knowledge. The status of wisdom or prudence as a *virtue* (http://en.wikipedia.org/wiki/virtue) is recognized in *cultural* (http://en. wikipedia.org/wiki/cultural), *philosophical* (http://en.wikipedia.org/wiki/ philosophical), and *religious* (http://en.wikipedia.org/wiki/religious) sources. Some define wisdom in a *utilitarian* (http://en.wikipedia.org/ wiki/utilitarian) sense, as foreseeing consequences and acting to maximize the long-term common *good* (http://en.wikipedia.org/wiki/goodness).

As such, in general, wisdom is looked at as a person's ideals, the principles that govern all of his or her actions and decisions. Applications of personal wisdom include the ethical and social guidelines that determine a person's unique style of personality, the particular nature of short- and long-term goal(s) pursued (spiritual or materialistic for example), and the person's perspective on life, social attitudes, *etc.*

Well, Ms. Wise, there you have it—the answer to your question at last. Please don't thank me; I am not used to flattery. May I be of any further assistance to you?

> Ms. Wise:
> The Eagle soars in the summit of Heaven,
> The Hunter with his dogs pursues his circuit.
> O perpetual revolution of configured stars,
> O perpetual recurrence of determined seasons,
> O world of spring and autumn, birth and dying!
> The endless cycle of idea and action,
> Endless invention, endless experiment,
> Brings knowledge of motion, but not of stillness;
> Knowledge of speech, but not of silence;
> Knowledge of words, and ignorance of The Word.
> All our knowledge brings us nearer to our ignorance,
> All our ignorance brings us nearer to death,
> But nearness to death no nearer to God.
> Where is the Life we have lost in living?
> Where is the wisdom we have lost in knowledge?
> Where is the knowledge we have lost in information?

G: From T.S. Eliot's *Choruses from the Rock* (1934). I'm impressed, Ms. Wise; you are not as ignorant as you look.

W: Mr. Google, forgive me for saying this, and I don't mean to sound impertinent, but I don't think you get it.

G: Get what, Ms. Wise?

W: All your answers, what you have provided me so far…all you seem to be able to provide me with in your self-declared omniscience is information and more information. But as the poet says, "Where is the wisdom we have lost in knowledge? Where is the knowledge we have lost in information?" Can you answer me that?

G: I am sorry to sound unhelpful, Ms. Wise, but I just don't know what you mean.

W: That's the problem, Mr. Google. That is precisely the very heart of the problem: I am asking you for meaning, and all you can provide is more information. The point is, you know, that I just don't know how to use all that information in attaining wisdom so as to have a good life and attain happiness—the holy grail of ancient Greek philosophy, no less. After all, what's the good of all this information if it can't show you how to be wise and happy, hmm? Answer me that!

G: Wisdom shmisdom—that's all everyone wants. What's wrong with just a few plain facts? Or as many as you can possibly store within your limited brain's capacity. Isn't that enough? You can be wise with that, you know. Data, my dear girl, data, big data—that is all that counts.

W: No, Mr. Google, that's where you are wrong. I can't be wise with the mere accumulation of data. Certainly facts and information are all very useful and necessary as a first step to becoming wise, for willful ignorance is no friend of the wise. But it is simply not enough. One must first turn data into meaningful information and information into knowledge. And knowledge, as you must surely know, is justified true belief. And finally, by learning how to use one's knowledge adequately and appropriately in finding what constitutes a good life and living such a life, one attains wisdom and happiness. For only the good can be wise and the wise happy. At least that's the theory...(Ms. Wise turns to the audience with a genuine expression of doubt) isn't it?

G: I am not a philosopher, Ms. Wise, though I dare say I know more than all the philosophers that ever lived, now live, and will ever live—put together. My knowledge is infinite and enduring, whereas theirs is limited and ephemeral, like the hairs on their heads. Have you noticed how many bald philosophers there are?

W: Mr. Google, even if I were to agree with you that you have limitless information at your fingertips, as you seem to have, that is not knowledge. You have no way of knowing whether any of that is true or reliable. It may be useful at a trivia night down at the pub or on a TV Quiz show, but none of it amounts to an iota of knowledge until its possessor knows it to be true. To put it simply, you have to know that the information at your disposal is in fact true and justified; you have to know that you know! Information just by itself is data, Mr. Google, not knowledge. Meaningful data, perhaps, well-formed and well-organized data, perhaps, but data nevertheless.

It is human intelligence and understanding that transforms information and data into knowledge. And that, Mr. Google, is your big failing, if I may say so. For all the trillions of gigabytes of information you have at your fingertips, it doesn't count for one gram of knowledge unless someone like me knows for certain that it is true. You may indeed have oodles more information than I have, but I have more knowledge: I am capable of knowing how much or how little of your information is true. I share that capability with the Creator. I, too, have eaten from the Tree of Knowledge:

The world turns and the world changes,
But one thing does not change.
In all of my years, one thing does not change,
However you disguise it, this thing does not change:
The perpetual struggle of Good and Evil.

(Eliot 1934).

G: Ms. Wise, I give you information to utilize and live a
           better life, and you choose poetry instead—that indeed is
           the height of folly. Where's the wisdom in that?

W: There's more wisdom in one true word of poetry than all
           the information at your command, Mr. Google. Good
           poetry is like philosophy: it does not lie; it points beyond
           itself to the intimate and serene spaces of eternal truth.

G: Words, Ms. Wise, empty rhetorical words. By the way,
           did you know that your Mr. T.S. Eliot also studied philos-
           ophy? No, you didn't know? Why does that not surprise
           me? You would rather be ignorant but wise.

W: In the beginning was the Word, Mr. Google.

G: *In the beginning was the Word, and the Word was with
           God, and the Word was God.* The Gospel of John 1:1.
           Now the word is me, Ms. Wise—lots of them—lots and
           lots of words. Why settle for one when you can have so
           many. You ask for the Word; I give you a trillion encyclo-
           pedias of words and Wikipidias besides. You can make
           up your own words and your own worlds if you wish—I
           have set you free, can't you see? *You* now are the creator!

W: Mr. Google, let me try once more: If the object of life, as
           Aristotle correctly put it, is to be happy, for who would
           knowingly choose to be unhappy, then isn't it essential
           that we know the means for its attainment? Isn't it possible
           that the best means for the attainment of happiness is the
           possession of wisdom, for it is only perhaps the wise that
           can be truly happy, knowing so well from history how folly
           leads only to disappointment at best, to misery at worst?

G: Ms. Wise, you don't need me; you need a psychiatrist.

W: You're not entirely wrong there, Mr. Google, for the real
           philosophers of Greek antiquity were in effect the first
           psychiatrists: they saw philosophy as the true physician
           of our souls. You're absolutely right then, Mr. Google; I
           don't need more information I have enough of that
           already—too much already. No, what I do need is
           therapy, therapy of the soul, and that, I am afraid, is what
           you can't provide. Thank you ever so much for making
           me realize that. I can't thank you enough. You have, even

if not intending to, shown me that information is not knowledge and knowledge not wisdom. You truly wouldn't know just how helpful you have been. Thank you, thank you, thank you, Mr. Google.

G: That's quite all right, Ms. Wise, quite all right. Glad to be of service. Please come and visit me again soon. Oops I must run; someone is asking for the recipe for *ratatouille*.

Wisdom Deficit in an Age of Information Abundance[1]

The above *philosophy play* is designed to highlight the difference between information, knowledge, and wisdom and how information and knowledge by themselves are not sufficient in securing and promoting our individual and collective well-being or happiness, which is the practical knowledge or "know-how" that wisdom alone provides. Moreover, the uncritical and unreflective dissemination and use of information far from securing and promoting our well-being can in some cases as we will examine below, damage us or others and make us unhappy. Cyberbullying and cyber-crime are two instances of such harmful productions and uses of information. In addition, as we have seen in examining the *Dual Obligation Information Theory* in Chapter 5 and its application in Chapter 6 and other chapters in this book, clearly demonstrates that for information to count as knowledge certain epistemic conditions such as truth or truthfulness must first be met. Information, however, that is true as a form of knowledge cannot of itself show us how to live well in securing and promoting our well-being as individuals and as society. For that we need wisdom, the knowledge of what constitutes a good and fulfilling life, one capable of promoting and securing the attainment of well-being and happiness for us and others.

The age of abundance of information is paradoxically marked by a deficit of wisdom. It seems that, the more information we have, the less wise we are in managing and controlling it for our individual and collective well-being. The problem is that there is too much information and not enough time to absorb it, understand its implications, and judge the best way to use it for our individual and common good. The glut of information has created gluttony for information, which can lead us to behave unwisely and sometimes foolishly. Examples of such unwise and foolish online behavior abound.

Take for example the Australian treble Olympic gold medalist Stephanie Rice (http://www.smh.com.au/sport/swimming/i-want-you-to-know-how-sorry-i-am-tearful-rice-20100908-150s3.html), who lost a lucrative sponsorship with Jaguar as a result of a thoughtless tweet about the South African rugby team; the Canberra Raiders star Joel Monaghan (http://www.smh.com.au/rugby-league/league-news/joel-monaghan-in-tears-after-quitting-the-raiders-20101109-17lff.html) who was photographed performing an act of simulated bestiality with a dog, which was later published on the Internet and forced his resignation; Catherine Deveny (http://www.smh.com.au/entertainment/tv-and-radio/deveny-dropped-as-columnist-for-the-age-20100504-u6si.html), a journalist with the *Age* who was fired for a series of unsavory but mostly silly tweets about various TV personalities and celebrities; a journalist photographer from Ireland who was sacked after making comments on her Facebook page about the young woman Michaela Harte (http://www.irishcentral.com/news/irish-photographer-sacked-over-hateful-michaela-harte-facebook-comments-114707754-237355381.html), who had been murdered on her honeymoon in Mauritius; American journalist Nir Rosen (http://www.news.com.au/world/journalist-nir-rosen-quits-after-insensitive-and-offensive-lara-logan-tweets/story-e6frfkyi-1226007376215), who had to resign after making offensive tweets about Lara Logan, the CBS journalist who was sexually attacked in the recent demonstrations in Egypt. More commonly still, young people undermine their privacy and chances of future employment by placing compromising photos of themselves and friends on Facebook and engaging in cyber-bullying that has allegedly driven young people to suicide. The problem is widespread and global.

There are countless daily informational acts of unwise and self-defeating behavior, which, but for the all-seeing-eye of the omnipresent Internet, would pass unnoticed as matters of no consequence. An important truth the WikiLeaks controversy has revealed is that the Internet and the digital informational environment affords no one the certainty or comfort of privacy. The Internet is, by its very nature, a boundary-free public space not well-suited to private conversations and secrets and, what's more to the point, informational indiscretions. The digitization of information has fundamentally changed not only the way we disseminate information but the way we live.

We are becoming informational beings increasingly spending our lives in the infosphere, where we play, pray, download and upload recipes, music, and movies, buy and sell, chat and live in virtual worlds, and make and break "friendships" at a click. The Internet, just like the natural environment, cannot be neatly constrained and controlled by any one group of individuals, conglomerates, or nations. And like the natural environment, the Internet is capricious and unpredictable and only favors the uninhibited free dissemination of information by anyone, anytime, and anywhere.

If we cannot control or manage the flow of information on the Internet, the next best thing is to control our own online informational behavior. That is within our control. We have to learn how to use and disseminate information wisely, in a manner that protects and promotes our individual and collective well-being. Wisdom that was the core concern of philosophy in ancient Greece and Rome—think of Plato, Socrates, Aristotle, Zeno, Epicurus, Epictetus, Seneca, and Cicero, Confucius in China, and the Buddha in India—provides a ready-made model. As a *higher-type of knowledge* (knowing how to understand and use information upon reflection and with good judgment for the benefit of oneself and society), wisdom can provide practical "know-how" for applying information to improve our lives and that of others. It is also a *reflective virtue* in the form of practical prudence, which can teach us how to create and use information to live good and meaningful lives in the infosphere—lives that are capable of leading to self-fulfillment, eudaimonia, and happiness for us and others. What wisdom requires is that we learn the husbandry of information. How to reflect upon it, how to understand it, how to control it so it does not control us, how to judge its implications so we can foresee its consequences, whether they are good or bad, and how to use it in ways that enhance our well-being and promote and protect our rights to freedom, privacy, and respect. In the age of information, it seems that we would be better off with more wisdom and a little less information. Switching over our iPhone and iPad to Plato, sometimes, may be a good start.

The Dual Obligation Information Theory-Wisdom Model

The *Dual Obligation Information Theory (DOIT)* model introduced in Chapter 5 and the related *Dual Obligation Information Theory-Wisdom* model (DOIT-Wisdom model) that we will examine in this section were developed for the purpose of normatively evaluating the dissemination of information at the convergence of old and new media and its impact on the good life or well-being of individuals and society generally. As a reminder, a summary of the DOIT argument appears below:

The communication of information as *informational action* has a dual inherent normative structure that commits all informational agents to general epistemological and ethical values and norms. The communication of information as *information* commits informational agents to certain communicative epistemic and ethical values such as truth, accuracy, truthfulness, honesty, reliability, and trustworthiness. In addition, the communication of information as informational *action*, commits information agents to respect for the universal rights to freedom and well-being of all other informational agents (Spence 2009 and Gewirth, 1996, 1978). This is the conclusion of the argument from DOIT we examined in detail in Chapter 5.

Wisdom, as a form of knowledge about what a good life is, the value of such a life, and how to actively pursue it and realize its attainment, is also a reflective meta-virtue whose possession enables the identification, evaluation, and application of first-order knowledge as information, for the active pursuit of the good life for its attainment (Spence 2011a).

Since wisdom requires information and knowledge oriented toward the realization of the good life, and since the acquisition and communication of such knowledge entails epistemic and ethical norms as well as eudaimonic values, values that relate to the pursuit and attainment of a good life and well-being, wisdom is therefore central and crucial to the evaluation of information, including digital information, and its relation to the good life. Hence the normative structure of informational action is shown to have a common and essential conceptual connection with wisdom with regard to the promotion of a good life for the attainment of eudaimonia, well-being, or happiness.

The extension of DOIT to include the notion of *wisdom* and in particular, practical wisdom (Spence 2011a), in the *DOIT-Wisdom* model allows for the evaluation of the impact of information, including digital information, on the well-being and happiness of citizens. This is particularly useful because *wisdom* provides a single direct conceptual link between information on the one hand and well-being on the other. Moreover and relatedly, the DOIT-Wisdom model is also capable of providing practical guidance to all informational agents, including journalists, for using digital information wisely, after proper reflection, and with good judgment for the good of themselves and that of others.

The following is a diagrammatic and visual representation of the *DOIT-Wisdom Model*:

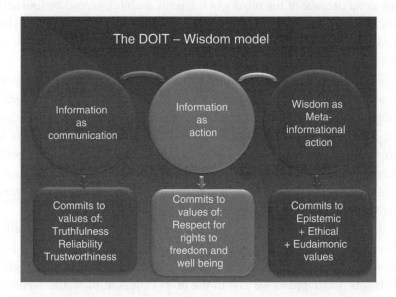

Source: Spence, Edward 2009. Reproduced with permission of Springer

Communicating Wisely

In an age where information is a valuable marketable commodity, we need ethical journalism more than ever. We also need the inculcation of an ethical culture. Ethics and its essential twin subject, epistemology, the philosophy of knowledge, are at the heart of good journalism. The reason for this is quite simple. Since the primary role of journalism is the truthful, accurate, balanced, and fair dissemination of information for the public interest (the epistemology of information), journalists are committed by virtue of that role to certain unavoidable ethical commitments, such as truthfulness, honesty, trustworthiness, a sense of fairness, and moderation, as well as a commitment to what best serves the public interest.

Public interest is not what is often confused as "of interest to the public." The latter at best feeds the unwholesome curiosity of readers who are more interested in gossip than worthwhile news. The *News of the World* case examined in Chapter 6 undermined the public interest rather than promote it. If truth is the first victim of war, privacy is the collateral damage of the misuse of the term "public interest" by journalists. Even when it serves the public interest, the right of the public to be informed should be balanced with the right to privacy. The former does not automatically override the latter.

The ethical dissemination of information by journalists requires both knowledge and wisdom in the form of reflection, understanding, and judgment in knowing when and how journalists are to apply knowledge for both professional and public good. Wisdom is essential because it provides practical guidance for how to act for the enhancement of both personal and social well-being. Wisdom is the lighthouse for a meaningful and well-lived life both offline and online, as we now live increasingly in the "infosphere."

Rules alone don't work because often they seem imposed externally. They come across as punitive and can be easily broken if there's nothing more fundamental to support them other than the fear of being caught. This was illustrated as we saw in the cases of Jayson Blair and Stephen Glass, examined in Chapter 9. Principles and virtues, by contrast, are internally generated through the cultivation of reflective thinking that empowers rather than alienates. That is because the commitment to them emanates internally from the communicators of information themselves, through their own rational reflective thinking. As Aristotle rightly observed, thinking is our most basic and essential human attribute. And as the French seventeenth-century philosopher Blaise Pascal (https://en.wikipedia.org/wiki/blaise_pascal) profoundly remarked: "All our dignity consists in thought. It is on thought that we must depend for our recovery, not on space and time, which we could never fill. Let us then strive to think well; that is the basic principle of morality" (Pascal, 1995). Ethics involves clear, rational, and reflective thinking: wise thinking. Good thinking also helps cultivate and civilize emotions—what David Hume, an eighteenth-century Scottish philosopher, called the moral sentiments (Hume, 1998).

In the age of Google, the skills of description have become nothing more than a cut-and-paste exercise of information gathering. It requires little, if any, reflective thinking or judgment of how to evaluate and apply information wisely for one's personal and professional good or for the public good.

Lee Wilkins correctly points out that, in addition to their traditional role of informing the public, journalists should also seek to mitigate harm to the public. To do so, she says, the definition of news should not only include what actually happens but also *what might happen*. As Wilkins eloquently puts it, "preventing harm becomes the predominant ethical obligation" of journalists (2010, 313). Journalists should become what she calls "mitigation watchdogs." Wilkins' argument for mitigation reporting, in principle if not intent, dovetails the argument for communicating wisely, for it is through thinking and acting wisely as communicators that journalists not only mitigate harm but also promote well-being for the individual and public good.

What should guide legacy and digital journalists in the twenty-first century and beyond are the principles of truth, trust, reliability, justice, and wisdom. The information they disseminate on matters of public interest should be for the public good. To that end, journalists of the information age must not only seek the truth but also act wisely in communicating it. For if wisdom is understood as the knowledge of what a good life is and how to live such a life for the enhancement of individual and societal well-being, then it is also in the public interest—a public interest that journalists of both the fourth and fifth estates should promote. In addition to becoming Lee Wilkins's mitigation watchdogs, journalists should also become "wise watchdogs" in promoting societal well-being through the communication of truthful, reliable, and trustworthy information, which is clearly also in the public interest.

Questions for Reflection

1   *What is wisdom and why is it essential for the dissemination of information?*
2   *What are the differences, if any, between information, knowledge, and wisdom, and why do they matter?*
3   *Was Ms. Wise, in the philosophy play, wise to seek wisdom from Mr. Google? Was that a good starting point? Can we learn what wisdom might be by first learning what it is not?*
4   *Search and find a case study of misinformation or disinformation and apply the DOIT-Wisdom model in analyzing and assessing its Epistemic, Ethical, and Eudaimonic implications.*

Note

1   This section is based on an earlier published version; see Spence (2011b).

Works Cited

Eliot, T.S. 1934. "Choruses from the Rock". *The Complete Poems and Plays of T.S. Eliot.* London and Boston: Faber and Faber, 145–167.

Gewirth, A. 1978. *Reason and Morality.* Chicago, IL: Chicago University Press.

Gewirth, A. 1996. *The Community of Rights.* Chicago, IL: Chicago University Press.

Hume, D. 1998. *An Enquiry Concerning the Principles of Morals.* Oxford Philosophical Texts.

John, *Gospel of St John 1:1* New Testament, English Standard Version.

Pascal, B. 1995. *Pensées.* London: Penguin Classics.

Spence, E. 2008. *Wise After the Fact (Wisdom in the Informatrion Age).* A philosophy play performed for the Greek Festival of Sydney, Australia, Ithaka Kefeneion, April, 14, 2011.Accessed April 5, 2017. www.greekfestivalofsydney.com.au.

Spence, E. 2011a."Information, Knowledge and Wisdom: Groundwork for the Normative Evaluation of Digital Information and Its Relation to the Good Life." *Ethics and Information Technology* 13 (3): 261–275.

Spence, E. 2011b. "IT Savvy, but Stupid." *Australasian Science* May 32 (4).

Spence, E. 2009. "A Universal Model for the Normative Evaluation of Internet Information." *Ethics and Information Technology* 11 (4): 243–253.

Wilkins, Lee. 2010. "Mitigation Watchdogs: The Ethical Foundation for a Journalist's Role." In C. Meyers (ed.), *Journalism Ethics: A Philosophical Approach*. New York, NY: Oxford University Press, 311–324.

Epilogue
Digital Diversity and Democracy

The Universal Declaration of Human Rights (http://www.un.org/en/universal-declaration-human-rights/) was signed more than 50 years before anyone had even conceived of the Internet. But that first world-wide expression of human rights laid the foundation for freedoms that the Internet has made finally possible for people to attain. Article 19 of the Declaration reads: "Everyone has the right to freedom of opinion and expression; this right includes freedom to hold opinions without interference and to seek, receive and impart information and ideas through any media and regardless of frontiers." Article 20 reads: Everyone has the right to freedom of peaceful assembly and association. The Internet made it possible to "seek, receive and impart information and ideas." It made it possible for people to assemble and associate across any borders or boundaries. Universal accessibility to the Internet has been called the freedom to connect (https://www.youtube.com/user/F2Cconference).

This concluding chapter stresses the importance of Internet inclusion for all people. The web-based worldwide experiment in connection, communication, collection of opinion and deliberation has been effective. Twenty-first century movements could not have occurred without digital connection. These include the Occupy Movement (https://en.wikipedia.org/wiki/Occupy_movement), 15-M movement (http://revolution-news.com/social-movements-spain-15m/), as well as the Arab Spring

Ethics for a Digital Era, First Edition. Deni Elliott and Edward H. Spence.
© 2018 John Wiley & Sons Ltd. Published 2018 by John Wiley & Sons Ltd.

(http://middleeast.about.com/od/humanrightsdemocracy/a/Definition-Of-The-Arab-Spring.htm) uprisings.

Civic discourse, which is the freedom to speak and listen to ideas, is necessary to sustain democracy. The tools to share information are theoretically in the hands of every individual who has access to the Internet. That is both the good news and bad news. It is good news because digital connection has led to decentralization of communication and empowered every person to contribute. It is bad news because wealthy corporations and the world's citizens who have the highest income, education, and employment are overwhelmingly those who have Internet access and who usually shape virtual conversation. Those disenfranchised by poverty, illiteracy, disability, gender and geography are more often voiceless or are not heard over the polished professional messages provided by those with profit or other self-interest in mind.

According to the International Telecommunication Union (ICT) Facts and Figures for 2015 (http://www.itu.int/en/ITU-D/Statistics/Documents/facts/ICTFactsFigures2015.pdf), the digital divide is narrowing, but Internet use still favors those in developed countries. In 2005, 16% of the world's population had Internet access; in 2015, that had jumped to 40% of the population. But, while 78% of those in developed countries used the Internet, only 32% of the population in developing countries did so. Three-g mobile-broadband availability expanded by 2015 to cover 69% of the world's population, with greatest coverage in urban areas (89%) as compared with rural areas (29%). Mobile broadband has been a significant force in connecting the world's people as mobile is less expensive than fixed broadband and is portable. Many important events have gained worldwide attention because of real-time broadcasts through hand-hold devices.

Digital inequity reflects and reinforces other disparities. In a world increasingly dependent on digital communication, those without access are even more isolated than they might have been if they received even outdated physical-news products. Just as water, food, and shelter provide the minimum elements for individuals' bodies to thrive, access to information provides individuals and groups with a basis from which to evaluate their own context in comparison with others. Knowing channels of communication allows for individuals' civic power to emerge. The only way to ensure that all perspectives are represented is 100% global penetration. Digital technologies create new interactions that influence the physical world. But, providing hardware, software, and basic computer literacy is not enough.

Digital Cultures (http://culturalpolitics.net/digital_cultures) is one of many web-based organizations focused on the cultural digital divide. According to that web site, "Significant lack of representation and mis-representation of particular racial, ethnic, and cultural groups in the media has long been shown to have profound negative psychological effects on the groups. In turn, this misrepresentation has strongly adverse implications for social justice and equitable social policy because of the broad consumption of these media by the general public and policy makers." Digital Cultures encourages technical training for mem-bers of underserved groups. "These culturally competent technically savvy individuals can then work as facilitators for marginalized commu-nities to empower them to represent themselves in digital media on their own cultural ground via their own cultural forms." Only those who are themselves within a group can attest to the authenticity of the repre-sentation of that group.

Put another way, storytellers have their own cultural blinders. For example, the American-generated narrative regarding the 7.2 earthquake in Kobe, Japan in January 1995 that killed more than 5,000 people and injured more than 10 times that number told a story of Japanese inefficiency and inaction. Writing from an American perspective of how one's government should respond to a major natural disaster, American journalists wove shock and disgust into their narratives as they reported that foreign offers of supplies, volunteers, and second-hand clothes were rebuffed (Elliott 1997).

For example, Markman (1995a) reported in the *Los Angeles Times*:

Americans volunteered "in the belief that Japan needed trauma-care specialists to assist in the treatment of the Kobe earthquake's 50,000 wounded. Upon arrival in the city, however, the gung-ho emergency room doctors and nurses discovered that their Japanese counterparts had a much more narrow view of volunteerism. ... Their arrival was a bit clumsy, as Japanese health executives tried to figure out how to accommodate col-leagues whom they considered guests more than assistants. ...[E]mer-gency room chief Jung Hyo Kim ... drew the line of his welcome at the notion of asking the Americans to help out with rounds or in the operating room" (p. B3). Japanese doctors felt that the cultural differences were too great for American doctors to treat Japanese citizens effectively.

Three weeks after the earthquake, an American offer to fly as many as 1 million doses of flu vaccine to Kobe within forty-eight hours, free of charge, was politely declined by the Japanese Health and Welfare Ministry. At that point, search teams and undertakers, airlifts of food and clothing had also been refused. Two weeks after the earthquake, fourteen forklift pallets of Tylenol sent by one American relief organization had been left untouched in a warehouse near Kobe (Kristof 1995).

American citizens were horrified by what seemed to them to be a callous lack of response and gratitude from the Japanese government. The Japanese point of view was different. The view from Japan was that it had all of the help and supplies that it needed to cope with became known as the Great Hanshin Earthquake. Medicines packaged for Euro-Americans were not appropriately dosed for Japanese people with their smaller bodies and different metabolic tolerances. Culturally, Japanese people recoiled from "second-hand" clothing or materials not in original packaging. Japan, as a well-developed nation, had medical personnel, disaster response teams, and their own triage for how to help their citizens in need. Sudden arrivals of foreign people and materials only distracted attention from where it was needed, particularly with the long-standing Japanese tradition of politely welcoming guests. Consider how US officials and disaster response teams would have reacted if the Japanese response to the 9/11 terrorists attacks had been to send uninvited competent professionals to make sure that the Americans responded to the crisis correctly.

The Japanese response to the earthquake reflected contemplation, collaboration, and consensus rather than the quick dramatic, but some-times chaotic, action Americans had come to expect. Empirical analysis of global disaster response does not indicate that one or the other style results in more lives saved. But, the story told without cultural under-standing or sensitivity created negative judgments about the Japanese because of the American narrative frame (Elliott 1997).

Internet accessibility in one's own cultural terms extends beyond nations and ethnicities to include ethnicity, race, class, gender, and (dis)abilities in one's social identity. Accessible online communication provides an important information source for people with disabilities.

Text-to-speech and alt. descriptive programs for visuals allow people who are blind to access information far more easily online than in the physical world. People with any social identity different from the norm can participate in online classes and discussions without prejudice getting in the way of how others take in their messages.

Diversity is important because the truth of any issue or event is best told from the multiple perspectives of different people reflecting their various backgrounds, cultures, and experiences. According to media scholars Eric Deggans, "One of the consequences of media diversity for white news consumers is that they will see more columns, commentary and stories created from those perspectives, which can feel so different from their own. As the expanding world of digital media brings new voices into journalism's mix, traditional news values can be an invaluable guide for news outlets providing coverage to meet this cultural moment. The challenge to traditional journalism is to embrace new voices, bringing new perspective, ideas and values to news coverage, while keeping the accuracy, ethical conduct and fairness required by top-notch reporting" (Deggans 2014).

In exchange, Internet-propelled democracy invites minority members to create messages that penetrate cultural barriers. According to scholar Meira Levinson, "The kinds of civic skills and attitudes that young people need in order to become empowered democratic actors vary depending on the individual and community context. Minority students and communities may need to be able to codeswitch from Black Vernacular English to Standard American English, from religious to secular language, or from cultural references that are familiar only to the minority group to those that resonate with the majority group as well. The ability to shift like this is a key to acquiring and exercising power effectively in a democracy based on majority rule, but it is not an easily standardized goal or practice" (Levinson 2012, 279).

The old paradigm of news reporting rested on the belief that news was out there somewhere, waiting for enterprising journalists to discover it. Once discovered, journalists were thought to have the obligation to carefully and gingerly pry the news loose so that it could be delivered to audiences without journalistic framing, interpreting, or interfering with the ability of audience members to understand the news item in raw form. Journalists were expected to provide "objective" reporting.

News is now understood to be a rich, though complicated, combination of how journalist-facilitators gather data from a multitude of sources, including users, and how, through collaboration and inclusion, stay on top of what users need and want to know as a story progresses or multiple angles of the story emerge.

The journalistic intent, whether expressed through legacy news media or any other self-proclaimed news site or multimedia storyteller is an act of sifting, aggregating, and reflecting.

Media scholar Monica Guzman has offered powerful examples for how news reporting can and should look in an Internet-propelled democracy. Top-notch reporting may no longer look like traditional news stories. For example, NPR's social media specialist, Andy Carvin emerged as a news leader in the 2011 reporting of the Arab Spring revolutions, but not through traditional means. He used those on the ground to shape their own story and crowd-sourced among those involved to verify truth. "Carvin spent time curating the information being shared on Twitter by people on the ground—highlighting it, distributing it, even tapping those same people to help verify it. Some voices he already knew. The ones he didn't, he scrutinized, engaging them if they seemed genuine and helpful." Guzman said, "By curating the Twitter collection thoughtfully and openly, Carvin gathered the most important on-the-ground reports, turned the random chatter into collected wisdom and gave that wisdom right back to the people who needed it most" (Guzman 2014). People on-site were informed by his reporting along with those watching from far away.

The Seattle Times, which won a Pulitzer Prize for its breaking news coverage of a shooting in November 2009, was largely successful because the reporting team used Twitter to encourage anyone who knew anything to participate in reporting the story. According to Guzman, "Not just editors in the newsroom or reporters in the city, but workers who saw police cars zoom by, neighbors who noticed something suspicious, newsies who'd caught an interesting report, and nervous residents who just wanted to know that they weren't alone." Guzman called the act of bringing together all of the voices is itself "an act of journalism." She said, "People are gathering in inclusive, open spaces to do what a new generation of online tools lets them do – inform themselves" (Guzman 2014).

The reporting of important information—acts of journalism—connect individuals across any number of differences with the goal that good journalism has always had: inform individuals so that they can effectively govern themselves.

Works Cited

Deggans, E. 2014. "How Untold Stories Can Reflect Diversity." In K. McBride and T. Rosenstiel (eds.), *The New Ethics of Journalism*. Los Angeles, CA: Sage.

Elliott, D. 1997. "The Great Hanshin Earthquake and the Ethics of Intervention." In F. Casmir (ed.), *Ethics in Intercultural and International Communication*. Englewood Cliffs, NJ: Earlbaum.

Guzman, M. 2014. "Community as an End." In K. McBride and T. Rosenstiel, *The New Ethics of Journalism*. Los Angeles, CA: Sage.

Kristof, N. 1995, February 4. "Japan Reluctant to Accept Help from Abroad." *The New York Times*, B1.

Levinson, M. 2012. *No Citizen Left Behind*. Cambridge, MA: Harvard University Press.

Markman, J. 1995, January 24. "Emotional Rescue Quake: Stymied by Japanese Reluctance to let Foreigners Treat Patients, Southland Medical Team Provides a Grief Therapy Session—and Kitchen Help—Instead." *The Los Angeles Times*, 1.

Index

Note: Page numbers in **bold** refer to figures, page numbers in *italics* refer to tables.

Ethics for a Digital Era, First Edition. Deni Elliott and Edward H. Spence.
© 2018 John Wiley & Sons Ltd. Published 2018 by John Wiley & Sons Ltd.